FROM RITUAL TO ART

*The Aesthetics and Cultural Relevance
of Igbo Satire*

Christine Nwakego Ohale

University Press of America,® Inc.
Lanham · New York · Oxford

Copyright © 2003 by
University Press of America,® Inc.
4720 Boston Way
Lanham, Maryland 20706

PO Box 317
Oxford
OX2 9RU, UK

British Library Cataloging in Publication Information Available

ISBN 978-0-7618-2485-5 (paperback)

DEDICATION

In Memoriam:

Boniface Nduka Oti
1945 - 1969

Vincent Agwuncha Oti
1915 - 1991

TABLE OF CONTENTS

FOREWORD

Important scholarly and literary work by Igbo women about Igbo people has been produced in the last few decades. Ifi Amadiume's sociological studies, Nkiru Nzegwu's editorial work on the journal *Jenda*, Chinwe Okechukwu's books of folktales, Benedetta Egbo's educational research, Buchi Emecheta's novels, Flora Nwapa's novels and short stories, Sister Joseph Agbasiere's anthropological study on women's associations, among so many others, have contributed to the efforts to understand African women's lives and to record and represent changing aspects of Igbo culture(s).[i] These women bring forth the points of view of Igbo people from all walks of life as they comment, sometimes wryly, sometimes with restraint, but always passionately, about how and what it means to live in an era of colonization and its after effects. Christine Ohale's work which you are now holding in your hands is another extraordinary document of the lives of Igbo people and especially Igbo women, in this case as a collective repertoire of satirical oral literature.

The strength of collectivity in Igbo women's communities cannot be underestimated. Indeed, African women in general should never be underestimated, despite the relative paucity of published works representing their words, thoughts and deeds. One thing that comes forth in Ohale's work is that Igbo women performers of all ages have been there with the men all along.[ii] Women have traditionally had a strong hand in creating, performing and passing along Igbo satirical song. Reading Ohale's book, one can envision the performances of archetypal satire by unmarried girls in Ihiala in eager anticipation of the *Ida Ji*, or Yam festival, just as easily as one can imagine an older and more accomplished woman singer grasping the complex power of satire to name names in order to sustain a lengthy and hilarious invective against the object of lampoon. These songs speak greatly about women's power to regulate social mores and several songs even entail controlling the behavior of wayward men.

Although individual performers of satirical song can and do exercise invention, as with other oral forms, the collective nature of these works transmits them through the ages. For at least hundreds of years, Igbo women and men have remembered and repeated rhyme, rhythm, onomatopoeia, and metaphors as well as the forms of these poems. Not only are the formal and poetic elements of the songs aides-de-mémoire, but the poems themselves are a form of collective memory and transmittal of culture; this aspect of the oral tradition provides both formal aesthetic continuity and social continuity across the generations.

But Ohale also is capturing a transformation of traditional satirical art forms of Igbo people from Ihiala. She has seen that these songs and their performance milieu are not yet completely gone (and may never ultimately disappear) but that as their social sanctioning functions have been supplanted by modern courts, prisons and monetary fines, their forms have shifted subtly. Her work to document that change provides to us a bridge between performances of the past and those of the present. In that way, Ohale contributes not only to the field of Igbo studies and African oral literature in general, but she has also given Igbo women the very latest word on the study of the development of oral history, oral performance and satire begun in antiquity. Satire is indeed a neglected field in African literary studies, and for bringing it forth and contextualizing its importance, we also owe Christine Ohale a debt that I hope will be repaid by much further study.

What of the neglect of satire as a field of study in African languages and literatures? Signifyin' is a much celebrated notion, as is the notion of the trickster figure.[iii] Both are studied widely in the literary achievements of Africans but there are other often humorous, always multifarious literary forms that have gone largely unexplored. Perhaps this is yet another after effect of colonialism in which Western researchers are only now coming to realize that the rich literature and performances of Africa involve sophisticated forms of satire.

Whenever an Igbo speaker takes the floor, it just might be said that a listener can anticipate moments of hilarious and complex satire. It is a pervasive form that extends beyond ritual performance into daily life. This is not to say that Igbo folks are unserious; if anything, Ohale's work shows how serious satire can be. It is especially so when sanctioning or providing social and aesthetic commentary on societal problems like teen pregnancy or inconstant providers to the family. She also shows how satire is serious to performer and audience in the transmission and appreciation of Igbo culture. So perhaps satire has also remained relatively unexplored because it is so prevalent. We may be unable to see the proverbial forest for the trees, at least until now. I believe that Ohale's work therefore will help researchers: to outline the elements and formal properties of satirical performance; delineate its typology in Igbo aesthetic terms as well as in the studies of satire begun in Juvenal's time; and track its transformations from a means of carrying out justice to an aesthetic and performative act. Ohale has taken us far in the study of satire and her book should help foster more studies on this vast and vital topic in a manageable paradigm.

Before leaving the reader to enjoy the volume, I will say a few more things about the value of this work. These poems, songs, and performances are all literary treasures to which Ohale does extraordinary historical justice. Ohale's contextualization of them will help current and future generations to understand how literature is embedded in social life. For example, she provides a history of Ihiala town, a succinct and brilliant discussion of how powerful magical words become aesthetic words in changing social systems, and an extraordinarily valuable collection of Ihiala songs with translations. Altogether, these chapters directly document how remarkable literary accomplishments arise directly from human social relations. Furthermore, the non-Igbo reader can begin to appreciate the brilliance of a song about how "a goat will rescue" a wayward husband! Certainly, as Ohale points out, when one puts an oral performance of a satirical piece in an African language into written English much escapes us – the cadence and rhythm of the dance that accompanies the songs, audience call and response, the lively tonal puns of the Igbo language, and the subtlety of Igbo worldviews derived from upbringing and fluency in the language. But now these songs are accessible to an order and a degree not previously possible. Our understanding grows wider today across Igbo and English speaking audiences and also among readers of the future. This does a great justice to the women of Ihiala (and their men) and to all African and non-African women whose voices were lost before someone had the foresight to record them.

Rachel R. Reynolds
Philadelphia, September 2002

---

[i] Amadiume has several books in print about African women. The journal *Jenda* is available on-line at http://www.africaresource.com/jenda. Okechukwu's books are

sometimes difficult to find, but a few are currently available from www.africabookcentre.com. Works by both Emecheta and Nwapa are widely available across the world. Routledge published Agbasiere's book *Women in Igbo Life and Thought* in the year 2000, and Egbo's study of poor women and literacy was based on fieldwork in Igboland. It is called Gender, Literacy and Life Chances in Sub-Saharan Africa, published in 2000 by Multilingual Matters. Nina Mba, although not herself Igbo, did a series of important studies with Clara Osinulu on women in Nigeria in general, such as *Nigerian Women in Politics 1986-1993*. Elizabeth Isichei has also done work on Igbo society and Nigerian oral history.

[ii] There have been a number of monographs and special edited volumes on Igbo language and culture, especially those sponsored by the now defunct Society for the Promotion of Igbo Language and Culture. They are for the large part devoted to studies of men or of Igbo societies in general, representing a male perspective. Ohale's book also continues the vitally important work of studies in language and culture, while addressing the need for more detailed studies on Igbo women's performance. For classics of Igbo studies, see Ogbalu, F.Chidozie. and Emenanjo, E. 'Nolue. *Igbo Language and Culture*, Vol. 1 and 2. Ibadan, Nigeria: University Press Limited. There are also other works on this topic by D. I. Nwoga and M. Echeruo in the works cited within this volume.

[iii] From the work of Henry Louis Gates.

PREFACE AND ACKNOWLEDGMENTS

Satire is such a prevalent activity that virtually everyone has been involved in it at least at some point. Yet, satire is one of the least studied genres of traditional verbal arts in Africa; it is a fertile ground that African literary scholars have tended to be slow in cultivating. Igbo satire scholarship has been particularly affected by this slowness. It is important at this point to find a lasting means of preserving this aspect of traditional literature not only to save the performances from total extinction but also to ensure that this art reaches a wider audience. This book is an attempt to address this need; it traces the development of Igbo satire from its origins in ritual to its literary use as an art form. In tracing this development, the author has analyzed the early form of Igbo satire and the factors that helped to change the context in which it was practised. Evidently, entertainment was not the sole objective of satire in early Igbo practice; satires were ritual practices which served many functions for the people and were never meant merely to entertain an audience. But events in Igbo history have helped to change the purpose of the ritual practices from their traditional utilitarian functions to entertainment.

The paradigm is Ihiala, an Igbo town in Anambra State of Nigeria. The author has recorded, transcribed, and translated live performances of satires by the people of Ihiala, and has attempted a critical analyses of their predominant themes and techniques.

The investigation reveals that although the concept of a corrective social function for satire is apparent in the songs, satirical performers do not overtly attempt to reform the culprit; instead, their interest is centred on self-expression and in the entertainment and amusement of the audience.

In an effort to ensure an orderly and systematic presentation, this work is divided into seven chapters. Each chapter presents a full argument with regard to the concerns of the chapter. But the chapters are also interdependent, for arguments raised only briefly in some chapters are treated more exhaustively in others. Furthermore, each chapter builds upon the insights gained in preceding chapters and, whenever necessary, extends arguments developed in them.

Chapter one is an introductory chapter which seeks to establish the background of the work and clarify its intentions. It discusses concepts related to satire since satire can be mistaken for other forms of art and literature. An attempt has been made to distinguish these other forms from satire to maintain clarity in the work. The chapter further discusses the early manifestations of the genre and the ultimate influence of Horace and Juvenal on the satirical practice.

Chapter two extensively reviews existing material on African oral literature - a discipline that is yearning for systematic, scholarly research.

Chapter three focuses on the people of Ihiala, their traditions of origin, and the dominant culture traits that stand them out as a people. Some of the areas investigated include: their cultural attitude, their basic beliefs, their worldview and their efforts to ensure the continuity of their existence as a people.

Chapter four discusses the methodology.

Chapter five addresses the predominant themes of Ihiala satire; it explores the occasions that most frequently encourage the performance of satires, and reveals how the people use and appreciate their satires.

Chapter six investigates the development, transformation, and performance of Ihiala satire.

Chapter seven explores the formal traits employed by Ihiala satires and provides proof that the satires share sophisticated literary techniques with the satires of the other cultures of the world and, therefore, have literary merit.

Finally, a brief conclusion is drawn from the insights gained in the preceding chapters about the developments in Ihiala satirical practice.

I would like to pay sincere tribute to all of those who have provided encouragement during the early stages of this book. Foremost among them are my parents: my mother, Agnes Chinanuekpele Oti, for her total involvement in the work especially during the field trips and the many recording sessions; my father, Vincent Agwuncha Oti, for inspiring enthusiasm in me about the work and for arranging and ccompanying me to the preliminary interview sessions. Unfortunately, he passed on before the work was halfway done. The eternal teacher, he taught me to stand tall and to harness the power of the human spirit. I bless his memory.

I continue to cherish the academic expertise of Emeka P. Nwabueze who supervised my doctoral work. Special mention must be made of Dr. Rachel Reynolds for believing in this project; Ms. Elselena Irons for a painstaking secretarial assistance and for preparing the final camera-ready copy; Ms Robin Benny and Dr. Richard Milo for editorial assistance, and the faculty members of the English department at Chicago State University for graciously admitting me into their fold.

Finally and quite separately, I reserve my greatest expression of gratitude for my children: Tochi, Lechi, Ola, and Ugo, without whom none of this would matter.

CHAPTER ONE

INTRODUCTION
GENERAL OVERVIEW AND
DEFINITION OF CONCEPTS

African oral literature is a discipline that has been yearning for systematic, scholarly research. Although a reasonable quantity of work has been published on this subject since the 1800's or thereabouts, easy access to the materials has not been readily guaranteed. This stems from the fact that very often these materials have been granted refuge in barely known journals whose readership is small, and so is the appreciation of their content. The popular notion of Africa as an arid farmland with respect to indigenous literary traditions is still somewhat a reality to this day. Ruth Finnegan's expression of Burton's views about Africa over a century ago still represents that popular notion regarding literary traditions in Africa. Burton states that:

> The savage custom of going naked has denuded the mind, and
> destroyed all decorum in the language. Poetry there is none....
> There is no metre, no rhyme, nothing that interests or soothes
> the feelings, or arrests the passions...[1]

For some reason, the majority of those who would immediately wave away the above view as bordering on the extreme may not readily admit that literary activity could take place among non-literate peoples. Their ambivalence to this fact largely determines their attitude to the study of African oral literature.

Not too long ago, the greater percentage of the work done in this discipline has been that of foreign scholars "who have often applied to the discipline the prevailing theories of European folklore scholarship."[2] They based some of their theories solely on speculations rather than on careful analysis of field data.

The purpose of this book, therefore, is to examine, comprehensively and analytically, the development of Igbo satire from its origins in ritual to its literary use as an art form. It will also demonstrate how traditional Igbo satirical performance has been transformed from a censure tool into a form of social entertainment.

A definition of the term "satire" is necessary to ensure clarity and comprehension in subsequent chapters. Robert Elliott, concluding the preface to his book *The Power of Satire: Magic, Ritual, Art,* notes that:

> Satire is notoriously a slippery term, designating, as it does, a form
> of art and a spirit, a purpose and a tone - to say nothing of specific
> works of art whose resemblances may be highly remote.[3]

This protean nature of the term "satire" may render any exact definition of the word often inadequate. Here we shall examine how some eminent literary authorities have defined satire in order to see how they have established a common ground for its understanding and appreciation. Gilbert Highet, in *The Anatomy of Satire,* informs us that satire comes from the Latin word "satura" which means "full," and has subsequently come to mean "a mixture full of different things"[4] to many people. The *Encyclopaedia Britannica* defines satire as:

> A mocking spirit or tone that manifests itself in many literary genres
> but can also enter into almost any kind of human communication.
> Wherever wit is employed to expose something foolish or vicious to
> criticism, there satire exists, whether it be in song or sermon, in
> painting or political debate, on television or in the movies.[5]

One can deduce from this definition that wit is central to any discussion of satire. Satire's relation to the law has constantly played a major role in determining the forms satire takes and the methods it uses. For instance, when verse satires were banned in England during the Elizabethan era, the poets immediately resorted to a new form that would accommodate the satirical impulse. Under the leadership of Ben Jonson and John Marston, the poets emerged with something new: the "comicall satyre." This clearly demonstrates the hazardous nature of satire and its perennial conflict with the law.

In his own contribution to the utility of wit, Freud posits that from the dawn of civilization, society has constantly subjected the hostile impulses of human beings, including their sexual impulses, to "restrictions and repressions." As people grow more civilized, they realize that it is unethical to use abusive language. Freud states that wit developed out of such prohibitions. He further states that:

> Society... prevents us from expressing our hostile feelings in action; and hence, as in sexual aggression, there has developed a new technique of invectives, the aim of which is to enlist... (society) against our enemy. By belittling and humbling our enemy, by scorning and ridiculing him, we indirectly obtain the pleasure of his defeat by the laughter of the third person (i.e., society)... Wit permits us to make our enemy ridiculous through that which we could not utter loudly or consciously on account of existing hindrances....[6]

Having been brought into the service of satire, wit empowers the literary satirist to use the rhetorical tools that aid him in his work. Some of these are: irony, innuendo, burlesque, parody, allegory, indeed, all the devices of indirection which help the satirist to deliver what may be originally considered impolite and unacceptable. The point to remember here is that those devices that tend to make satire acceptable to polite society actually call attention to it and sometimes render it even more effective.

M.H. Abrams notes that the range of satire is very wide and that ridicule is its major weapon. He defines satire as:

> The literary art of diminishing a subject by making it ridiculous and evoking toward it attitudes of amusement, contempt, indignation, or scorn. It differs from the comic in that comedy evokes laughter as an end in itself, while satire "derides"; that is, it uses laughter as a weapon, and against a butt existing outside the work itself. That butt may be an individual (in "personal satire"), or a type of person, a class, an institution, a nation, or even ... the whole race of

mankind.[7]

The above definition shows that there is no restriction as to the choice and scope of satirical targets. Satire can be directed at an individual, a group, an ethnic group, or even the entire people of a nation, such as Okot p'Bitek's attack on Clementine in *Song of Lawino,*[8] or Wole Soyinka's depiction of Sidi's laugh at the old Bale in *The Lion and the Jewel,*[9] Swift's and Soyinka's attacks on their contemporary societies, Dryden's on certain politicians, Achebe's on Nigerian leaders, etc.

One may ask why ridicule is a major weapon in the practice of satire. We demean our satirical targets by ascribing ignoble characteristics to them. This way we seem to legitimize the need to control them. Ridicule has the potential to neutralize the power of the victim. It is usually directed at one who deviates from accepted norms of behaviour, appearance, etc., and is one of the most powerful of all forms of public disapproval. The effect of ridicule will vary from society to society depending upon the values of the society, and the importance it places on the opinions of others. Ridicule always hurts, but the hurt will increase in direct proportion as the culture tends to internalize behavioural sanctions. Ridicule may be painful, but the pain is a far cry from that felt by people who have a shame culture. To this group, ridicule may even be fatal, and to lose one's good name could be the nearest thing to death.

Robert Elliott in *The Power of Satire* offers an apologia in defence of satirists and their art, and defends them for intervening for the common good. According to him, satirists

> Fight under the banners of truth, justice, and reason; ... they attack none but the guilty, ... their mission is a purifying one, undertaken almost against their will for the public benefit.[10]

The above declaration implies that even the choice of a satirical target is a moral act. Northrope Frye's comment throws more light in this regard. By implication, he rules out invective and lampoon as mere weapons of destruction, and commits the true satirist to an impersonal level. He asserts that

> For effective attack we (satirists) must reach some kind of impersonal level, and that commits the attacker, if only by

implication, to a moral standard. The satirist commonly takes a high moral line.[11]

Jonathan Swift claims that satire is medicine rather than malice and that proper satire is actually an instrument of therapy. Very often, the satirist not only feels torn between the tensions of love and hate, but feels the overwhelming need to wound those for whom he feels affection.

> Like a despairing parent, he applies the verbal lash or the jeer as instruments of moral and social therapy. These are painful, but he hopes that they will in time bring about a wholesomeness that must compensate for the hurt.[12]

Sadly, this positive goal is often not taken into account in the criticism of satire, when critics tend to see little or no reason for its continued practice.

Satirists frequently arouse revulsion in order to stimulate corrective action or urge that what they find objectionable be stopped. They use words as weapons to wound members of their community who fall short of standard expectations of moral decency. Donatus Nwoga's definition of satire buttresses the point. In his turn, he defines satire as "a form of verbal attack directed against individuals or groups who have offended either through personal injury or through breaking the mores of the community."[13]

Satire makes its point by projecting sources and instances of failure in human conduct and institutions. Alexander Pope happily declares that his satire "heals with morals what it hurts with wit."[14] Actually, there is no evidence that Pope's claim has ever affected the reactions of satirical victims. But there seems to be a certain degree of humaneness behind the savage criticism of satire; the satirical impulse is humanitarian at its highest level. The pain which satire inflicts should be seen as a prelude to relief and cure. Gilbert Highet in *The Anatomy of Satire* reaffirms one of the core reasons that have helped to sustain satire. He maintains that satire "wounds and destroys individuals and groups in order to benefit society as a whole."[15] The general aim of the genre is to plead with man to return to his moral senses.

All satirists claim that their aim is to stigmatize crime or ridicule folly, and thus to aid in diminishing or removing it. They approach their criticism of individuals or society by ridiculing those aspects of human behaviour which go against the mores and laws guiding conduct. John Dryden in support of the above claim states that "The true end of satire is the amendment of vices by correction."[16] He goes on to say that the true satirist cannot be called an enemy to the offender just as the physician cannot be called an enemy to his patient, when he prescribes an aggressive therapy in lieu of surgery.

One can deduce from the foregoing that the general purpose of satire, and by implication, the purpose of the satirist is, as Elliott has summed up:

> To expose some aspect of human behaviour which seems to him foolish or vicious, to demonstrate clinically that the behaviour in question is ridiculous or wicked or repulsive, and to try to stimulate in his reader (or in Roman times, his listener) the appropriate negative response which prepares the way to positive action.[17]

Since the ultimate purpose of satirists is to correct society, satire, therefore, serves as a corrective measure for people who have sunk into the swamp of social misbehaviour. It aims at the improvement of society and the consolidation of the stabilizing values that sustain a community. The satirist uses this dreaded weapon to initiate awareness of the need for human improvement.

THE PARADIGM

Since the satirical songs of Ihiala will be used as the paradigm for this work, it is necessary to devote some attention to the concept of paradigm. For the purposes of clarity this study conceives of a paradigm as any example or model used as representative. *Webster's New World Dictionary* defines a paradigm as:

> An overall concept accepted by most people in an intellectual community, as those in one of the natural sciences, because of its effectiveness in explaining a complex process, idea, or set of data.

Although Thomas Kuhn has extensively treated the concept of the paradigm in *The Structure of Scientific Revolutions*,[18] yet Margaret Masterman claimed to be able to discern twenty-two different senses in which the term was used.[19] That notwithstanding, one can employ what Kuhn himself refers to as a "disciplinary matrix," that is, the ability to discern a way in which the term could be used which would make it sufficiently precise to be potentially illuminating. In other words, if we identify a community in terms of, say, the subject of its investigations, the reaction of the members to stealing, we should expect to find a considerable number of things held in common by the members of the community. Kuhn's notion of a paradigm is meant to direct our attention to those common factors, reference to which is required in explaining the behaviour of the members of the community.

Among the things that Kuhn wishes to isolate through the notion of a paradigm include "models." Agreement on models may be agreement either that a particular analogy, say, between one community and others, provides a fruitful heuristic to guide research, or that certain connections should be treated as identical.[20]

CONCEPTS RELATED TO SATIRE

Satire can easily be mistaken for other forms of art and literature, unless its emotional and moral effects are clearly defined and understood. Certain forms of literature seem to have much in common with satire. It is, therefore, necessary to define and discuss these forms in order to clearly distinguish them from satire.

INVECTIVE AND LAMPOON

Invective is a speech or written work which is denunciatory, abusive or vituperative. In literature examples of invective are to be found fairly evenly distributed in verse and prose, and it is closely associated with satire, lampoon and caricature. Many writers have employed invective for a variety of purposes, the commonest being to express dislike, disgust, contempt and even hatred. It is often directed against a particular person; occasionally against a class or group; against an institution; a scene; and on life itself.

As a mode of expression invective is very ancient. Archilochus (7th C. BC) had a reputation for being sarcastically witty in his writings of which only a few are in existence. Persius (AD 34-62) was influenced by Lucilius, and in his First Satire is fairly abusive of the inferior poets and decadent literary tastes of his period. But the greatest in the use of invectives in classical literature is unquestionably

Juvenal (1st C. AD), who wrote ferocious attacks on the vices and abuses of the Roman lifestyle. He was particularly savage at the expense of the rich, and of women - to whom he devoted his Sixth Satire in which women are compared unfavourably to many different animals.

Lampoon is a virulent or scurrilous form of satire. It is a gratuitous and sometimes unjust and malicious attack on an individual. Although the term came into use in the 17th century from the French, examples of the lampoon are found as early as the 3rd century BC in the plays of Aristophanes, who lampooned Euripides in *The Frogs* and Socrates in *The Clouds*. In English literature the form was particularly popular during the Restoration and the 18th century, as exemplified in the lampoons of John Dryden, Thomas Brown, and John Wilkes and in several other anonymous satires.

Invective and lampoon lack nearly all the central purposes and underlying idealism of satire, and although the nausea which they induce could easily be used by a satirist, their moral import is not satirical. Because satirists are considered teachers, satire must serve the ends of morality.

COMEDY

The classic conception of comedy, which began with Aristotle in ancient Greece of the 4th century BC and persists through the present, holds that it is primarily concerned with man as a social being, rather than as a private person, and its function is frankly corrective. The comic artist's purpose is to hold a mirror up to society to reflect its follies and vices, in the hope that it will, as a result, be mended. Here comedy is considered primarily a literary genre. The word comedy seems to be connected by derivation with the Greek verb meaning "to revel," and comedy arose out of the revels associated with the rites of Dionysus, a god of viticulture. The origins of comedy are thus bound up with vegetation ritual. Aristotle, in his *Poetics*, states that comedy originated in phallic songs and that, like tragedy, it began in improvisation. Though tragedy evolved by stages that can be traced, the progress of comedy passed unnoticed because it was not taken seriously.

When tragedy and comedy arose, poets wrote whichever form best suited their natural inclination. Those who were inclined to celebrate the actions of the great in epic poetry turned to tragedy. Poets of a lower type, who had set forth the doings of the ignoble in invectives, turned to comedy. The distinction is basic to the Aristotelian differentiation between tragedy and comedy which stipulates that tragedy imitates men who are better than the average, and comedy men who are worse.

For centuries, efforts at defining comedy were to be along the lines set down by Aristotle, which hold the view that tragedy deals with personages of high estate, and comedy deals with lowly types; that tragedy treats of matters of great public import, while comedy is concerned with the private affairs of mundane life. He is also of the view that the characters and events of tragedy are historic and so, in some sense, true, while the humbler materials of comedy are but feigned.

Whereas comedy expresses the characters of men in the ordinary circumstances of everyday life, tragedy expresses the sufferings of a particular man in extraordinary periods of intense emotion. The characters of comedy arrange themselves in a familiar sequence: a clever hero is surrounded by fools and similar characters. The hero dissimulates his own powers while exploiting the weaknesses of those around him. Implicit here is the propensity to make folly ridiculous, to laugh it out of countenance, which has always been a prominent feature of comedy.

Renaissance critics, elaborating on the brief and ambiguous account of comedy in Aristotle's *Poetics*, stressed the derisive force of comedy as an adjunct to morality. Tragedy teaches by means of pity and fear, comedy teaches by deriding things that are highly offensive.

FARCE

Farce is a comic dramatic piece that uses highly improbable situations, stereotyped characters, extravagant exaggeration, and violent horse play. Farce is generally regarded as intellectually and aesthetically inferior to comedy in its crude characterizations and implausible plots, but it has been sustained by its popularity in performance and has persisted through the Western world to the present. In farce, character and dialogue are nearly always subservient to plot and situation. The plot is usually complex and events succeed one another with almost bewildering rapidity.

Antecedents of farce are found in ancient Greek and Roman theatre, in the comedies of Aristophanes and Plautus, entertainments in which the actors played stock character types - such as glutton, greybeard, and clown - who were caught in exaggerated situations.

The term farce was first used in France in the 15th century to describe the elements of clowning, acrobatics, caricature, and indecency found together within a single form of entertainment. Such pieces were initially bits of impromptu buffoonery inserted by actors into the texts of religious plays - hence the use of the Old French word farce, "stuffing." French farce spread quickly throughout Europe, notable examples being the interludes of John Heywood in England in the 16th century. Shakespeare and Molière eventually came to use elements of farce in their comedies. Farce continued throughout the 18th and 19th centuries and into the 20th century and found new expression in numerous successful television comedy shows.

THE CURSE

From the dawn of history, among people of every stage of civilization, the curse has been one of the most common forms by which man attempts to exercise control over the other. Put simply, a curse is a wish in a magical or religious context - a wish expressed in words that evil may befall a particular person. Perhaps a distinction should be made between the public curse, the cursing of the enemies of the state at the opening of important public function, and the private curse, originating in personal hatred, envy, or outrage and directed usually at the downfall or punishment of the enemy.

Just as curses have played a more important role in the history of man than blessings, so private curses have always been preponderate over public. Although there is considerable literary evidence, the best testimony to the widespread belief of the ancients in the efficacy of the curse is the number of Greek and Roman curse - tablets which have been recovered. Many of these small metal tablets which have been dug up from graves or sea bottoms contain only the name of the enemy with a nail driven through it. The magical principle operative here implies that the name is no mere sign distinguishing one person from another. By a magical process of identification, the name is the person, and he who controls the name controls the man.

It is actually impossible to make a formal distinction between magical satire and the curse. Both have public as well as more obvious private manifestations. The threat of satire is invoked in treatises, just as from the beginning of historical time the threat of curses has been invoked.   Archilochus, the archetypal satirist, sometimes calls on the gods to effectuate his will.   Satirists and cursers and magicians of all kinds rely upon a magical use in the formulas "Let him be such-and-such" and "May he be so-and-so."   Both satire and curse may be lethal, whether they accord with justice or not.

Just as it is impossible to disentangle the magical curse from the religious curse, so it is impossible, except in extreme cases, to disentangle magical satire from either.   One or two distinctions may, however, be pointed out. Magical satire is frequently in verse, whereas the curse is in prose.   Since satire employs ridicule, it may be distinguished from the curse.   But while ridicule is associated with satire from the beginning, it is not at this stage central to it. Perhaps it is better to look at both curse and satire as relatively undifferentiated responses to the threats and the possibilities of a hostile environment. Behind them both is the will to attack, to do harm, to kill - in some negative way to control one's world.

SPELL

It means words uttered in a set formula with magical intent. The correct recitation, often with accompanying gestures, is considered to unleash supernatural power.   Some societies believe that incorrect recitation can not only nullify the magic but cause the death of the practitioner.

Excellent examples of spells are recorded from the earliest times and especially in Greco-Egyptian papyruses of the 1st to the 4th century AD.   These include both magical recipes involving animals and animal substances and also instructions for the rites necessary to ensure the efficacy of the spells. The language of spells is sometimes archaic and is not always understood by the reciter. This frequently archaic and esoteric vocabulary of incantations may represent in a symbolic sense the mysterious nature of spiritual power and in a practical sense the restriction of human access to it. Personal names are commonly used in spells by magicians to work good or harm upon individuals. This power is regarded in some societies as so strong that each individual bears two names - a "real" one that is kept a secret and an everyday title, through which no magic can be worked. Gods and spirits are commonly believed to have special magical names, known only to a chosen few.

SATIRE AND RITUAL

Satire, like all art, developed out of ritual and notable examples
are widely practised tribal dances that reenact memorable events.
When the hunters of a tribe return from a successful expedition, they
often reenact their achievements in dance. The dances embody
complex motives, but prominent among them is the element of
"mimesis," of imitating and celebrating the achievement. But if the
dance is repeated frequently, it becomes removed from the particular
hunting expedition which may have given rise to it, and becomes
generalized. The dance becomes a celebration, not of a particular
hunt, but of hunting. As soon as the dance has achieved this
hypothetical abstraction, it becomes available for a magical use. The
dance does not only take place after an exploit but in anticipation of
some major event; the dance which may have originated as a "re-
presentation," then becomes a "pre-presentation." It becomes mimetic
of something anticipated, rather than of something accomplished. The
emphasis of primitive magic is on the end to be achieved. Just as
magic is founded on belief, ritual will retain its peculiar potency only
so long as belief is unquestioned. As soon as doubt and skepticism
appear, the rite may continue to be practised but its function will be far
removed from what it originally was.

Satire as an art cannot develop so long as belief in its magical
power still reigns in people's minds. While it is thought of as curse or
spell, its primary mode of existence will be governed by the non-
rational and non-literary formal relations of magic. When belief in its
magical power has been brought under control, then, through the
creative act of the poet, satire may break out of the forms which have
restrained it and be free to develop in the ways appropriate to art.
Initially, the dancers in the ritual dance mentioned above were
"making" magic. They were "making" the death of the animal or of
their enemies but when the belief in the magical power has gone, the
makers, like the dance, become something else. They may become
performers and the dance, detached from the emotion which originally
prompted it, may become a thing to be watched. The dance may, at
this point, become art. The earliest forms of traditional African
satirical expression exist in rituals which still survive in Igbo practice.

SATIRE AND MAGIC

Magic is a ritual performance or activity believed to influence human or natural events through access to an external mystical force beyond the ordinary human sphere. It constitutes the core of any religious system and plays a central social role in many non-literate cultures. The techniques of magic have generally been interpreted as supposed means to specific ends, for instance, the ensuring of an enemy's defeat or the summoning of rain.

In its early manifestations satire was closely associated with magic and the satirist was thought to possess preternatural powers. Archilochus is the archetypal figure in the tradition. Archilochus was a 7th century BC poet believed to be the "first" Greek literary satirist. On his father's side, he was a descendant of a line of hereditary priests of the great Earth-Mother, Demeter, and his mother was a slave. His engagement to Neobule, the daughter of a Parian noble failed to receive the expected approval by her father, Lycambes. This so enraged Archilochus that he composed iambics against the father and his household which he recited at the festival of Demeter. As a result, Lycambes and his daughter hanged themselves. Archilochus' satire killed, and indeed all satire "kills" symbolically. Lycambes and his daughter were believed to have been driven to suicide by the supernatural power of Archilochus' poetry.

Satirists have a variety of ways of achieving their malefic ends. Some of them achieve this by just uttering their invectives, others by calling upon their gods to destroy their enemies, and still others by performing certain magical rites in addition to the invectives. The different practices imply different sources of power. The resolution of the distinctions is for the anthropologists to decipher but it has been difficult for them to agree on an adequate terminology to deal with the complex problems arising from the belief in supernatural power and the attempts to control it.

The iambic verses of a major poet were believed to exert some kind of malefic power. This power seems to reside in the character of the poet and in his command over his utterances. It is difficult to tell whether the punishment of Lycambes and Neobule, precipitated by the iambic verse, actually brought about their deaths. Whether they lived or died is another matter. The point is that for a long time Archilochus' triumph over Lycambes commanded belief. This is what makes Archilochus' story relevant. It is crucial for an understanding of the image of the satirist as it develops over time, and as it exists today.

EARLY MANIFESTATIONS OF SATIRE

Satire is generally believed to have started in Rome. Aristotle traces the origin of comedy to the invectives, the iambics, and the satirical comments of the leaders of the Phallic Songs. Horace, writing of Lucilius, the man generally believed to be the "first" Roman satirist, maintains that Lucilius' writings were modelled after those of the writers of Old Comedy. During this period, comedy was categorized as Old and New. Old Comedy pokes fun at social, political, and/or cultural conditions as well as persons. Its characters are recognizable, contemporary personages. Contrary to the concerns of Old Comedy, New Comedy deals essentially with romantic and domestic situations, its popular characters being courtesans, lovers, and overbearing parents. Horace also talks about his own type of satire as deriving from Bion, the Greek philosophical preacher. There is, in addition, a well-known statement by Quintilian, a Roman rhetorician, which stipulates that satire is wholly a Roman phenomenon.

Every Roman poet of the Republican era was familiar with Greek and somehow was fascinated by the "grace and power" of Greek literature. It seems understandable that these poets may have been influenced, even if unconsciously, by a favourite Greek author. Yet satire is not usually thought to have existed in Greece. Satirical activity is as ancient as human history and the satirical spirit actually abounds in Greek literature from where Roman satirists possibly picked it up. The point is that there is no single word like "satire" to describe their literature.

The term "satura" has consistently been associated with the idea of "mixture." Juvenal's characterization of his own "saturae" incorporates all areas of human activity. By Quintilian's day, the form had become fixed and the tradition that Lucilius invented the form had become established. Although it is possible to see traces of Greek forms in the developed Roman satire, it is also true that Lucilius, and after him Horace and Juvenal, gave a structure to verse satire in a way that nobody had done before them.

Until Quintilian's time "satura" meant only a fraction of what satire means. It had no verbal or adjectival use as in "satirize" or "satirical." Gradually, "satura" came to signify a poetic form established by Roman practice. At that point the word yearned for expansion. The Romans readily found a Greek word of similar meaning and of almost identical form, "satyr," with a rich endowment of derivatives. These they appropriated to add to their existing "satura." The English term "satire" is derived from the Latin "satura" while "satirize" and "satirical" come from the Greek word for satyr, which in Greek society was usually associated with drama, and generally called the satyr play.

SATYR

The satyr play was a comical play involving a chorus of satyrs, mythological creatures who were half-goat and half-man. Structured like Greek tragedies, the satyr plays parodied the mythological and heroic tales that were treated seriously in tragedies. They poked fun at honoured Greek institutions, including religion and folk heroes, and often had a vulgar element.

INFLUENCE OF HORACE AND JUVENAL

The great Roman poets Horace and Juvenal established the distinctive features of formal verse satire and, as a result, influenced somewhat all subsequent literary satire. Although the Romans had definite ideas about what the social function of satire should be, yet there existed some conflict. Horace points out this conflict while reacting against an established satirical tradition. In his Fourth Satire he identifies Lucilian satire as performing the same function as Old Comedy. Horace's admiration for Old Comedy emanates from the fact that its writers criticized their targets with scathing severity. Roman criticism lays tremendous emphasis on the moral function of literature. Lucilian satire and Old Comedy both attack the wicked (usually by name) in the interests of social reform, and both forms of censure are bitter, biting, and witty. So the satirist is looked upon with a great deal of fear and suspicion in Horace's day.

Horace surprisingly opposes this dominant tradition. His former praise of Lucilius and of the writers of Old Comedy is undermined by his attack of Lucilius' style and by his characterization of his own satirical practice. His purpose is to initiate a new conception of the true nature of satire. As opposed to the harshness of Lucilius, Horace

attempts to give satire a milder nature and to infuse into it a richer
ethical content. His satire employs gentle mockery and playful wit and
he is so skillful about it that even his victim could laugh at himself.
The character in Horatian satire is urbane, witty, and tolerant and is
moved more to amusement than to indignation at the spectacle of
human depravation. Through his characterization Horace moves away
from the lacerating wit of Lucilius and his Greek forebears.

Persius, taking over from Horace, states a compelling drive to be
bold in his condemnation of the evils being perpetrated all around
him. His admiration of the writers of Old Comedy stems from the fact
that they boldly told the truth. Like Horace before him, Persius is
warned of the dangers that the satirist faces. The dangers are
undoubtedly real, constituting a kind of "occupational hazard." Even
at the height of its flowering, satire still received vigorous opposition.
Persius seems then to admire equally the approaches of both Horace
and Lucilius in their treatment of satire, the one treading cautiously,
and the other without restraint. The implication is that the two
approaches may actually be used to convey satire.

Juvenal completely opposes this whole idea. His conception of the
role of the satirist is completely different from that of Horace. He sees
himself as an upright man who is compelled to vent his frustration in
the midst of corruption and decay. Juvenalian satire, therefore, is
savagely derisive and convulses with hate at the corruption and evil of
human beings and their institutions. Juvenal makes known his reason
for undertaking the dangerous task of writing satire. He acknowledges
that hundreds of poets in his time write epics and tragedies but he
specifically chooses satire for a reason. He claims that no honest man
could sit and watch the corruption in Rome and do nothing to declaim
them.

Horace is of the opinion that satire should be rendered in everyday
language, the plain style being the appropriate medium. According to
ancient rhetorical theory, invective and abuse are associated with the
grand style, not with the plain style. Juvenal's invective and his
romance with the grand style carry him far beyond the prescriptive
bounds of the form as established by Horace. At the end of his Sixth
Satire, Juvenal asserts his innovation where he maintains that satire
has left the confines established by his Roman predecessors and has
taken the lofty tone of tragedy.

The conflicting practices of Horace and Juvenal have brought
confusing effects in the subsequent history of verse satire. Through

the ages both Horace and Juvenal have been elevated as the exemplars of "true" satire by eminent authorities, each arguing that his candidate is the model whose style should be adopted.

John Dryden wades into the problem in an effort to find a solution. His "Essay on Satire" revolves around the theoretical problems arising from the conflicting practices of Horace and Juvenal. Meticulously, he points out the merits and demerits in the two poets. Eventually, he proclaims that satire's affiliations were with comedy rather than tragedy, that it should laugh at evil, not declaim it. But Dryden admits that Persius and Juvenal changed satire for the better, claiming that certain vices require severe punishment rather than gentle reproof. For Dryden, Horace's deliberate choice of style was a choice which enabled Juvenal to excel. So Juvenal is associated with the "sublime" and the "majestic" while Horace is associated with the "low familiar way."

Dryden proclaims that Roman satire is of two kinds: comical satire and tragical satire. Horatian satire is associated with comedy while Juvenalian satire is associated with tragedy. Dryden maintains that the two poets in question equally excelled in their respective kinds. According to him, Horace lived in an age that demanded urbanity and good manners and to this he responded accordingly in his writing. Juvenal, on the other hand, was fortunate to live in a time of extreme corruption - a time that demanded censure, and lofty expression. Dryden, once again, sees Juvenal as responding appropriately to the demands of his age.

Juvenal lashed unmercifully at folly. So in the end Dryden takes a position: Juvenal's mode of satire is nobler than that of his predecessor, and he could consequently be considered the greater satirical poet. This final evaluation is somewhat misleading because Dryden sees all three poets as deserving victory in their individual satirical modes. John Dennis, writing some twenty years after the publication of Dryden's essay, argues that the comparison between Horace and Juvenal is unjust and is akin to comparing a tragic and a comic poet. It is significant that verse satire, as a result of the achievement of Horace and Juvenal, did become a literary form whose order and values were to be determined by reference to their practice.

From the times of Horace, Persius, and Juvenal, down to Boileau, Swift and Pope and to this day, satirists have corrected vices in society using the mode of satire that best appeals to them. Boileau, Dryden, and Alexander Pope, writing in the 17th and 18th centuries, seem to favour the Horatian tone. The Restoration and the eighteenth century loom large in satirical achievement.

NICOLAS BOILEAU

Nicolas Boileau was a poet and leading literary critic in his day, known for his influence in upholding classical standards in both French and English literature. In 1658 he began writing satires, attacking well-known public figures, which he read privately to his friends. After a printer had managed to obtain the texts and published them in 1666, Boileau produced an original version that he toned down considerably from the original.

His first satire is a monologue spoken by a beggar poet who is leaving Paris forever, since he cannot live and prosper there without becoming corrupt. This main theme and many of its subordinate developments are adapted from the Third Satire of Juvenal. Although he does not even mention Juvenal's name, Boileau's satire follows the footsteps of Juvenal.

JOHN DRYDEN

John Dryden's literary reign, crowned by the wreath of the poet Laureate in 1671, included several literary provinces. His great satire, "Absalom and Achitophel," was carefully planned to promote political reform. The particular vices that he wanted corrected were those of the Whigs of his day, who were seeking to secure the succession of the Duke of Monmouth, illegitimate son of Charles II, to his father's throne. The Earl of Shaftesbury and Monmouth and their supporters are keenly characterized and slashingly satirized. Realizing that direct satire might defeat its purpose by incurring resentment, Dryden chose to attack the Whigs by casting them as characters in the Biblical story of Absalom's revolt against David. To increase the effectiveness of the satire, he cast it in verse, "for there's a sweetness in good verse, which tickles even while it hurts."[21] But only a very daring satirist would venture to write a poem in which the monarch's

Vigorous warmth did variously impart
To wives and slaves; and, wide as his command
Scattered his maker's image through the land.[22]
(Absalom and Achitophel 8 - 10).

ALEXANDER POPE

Alexander Pope, like others before him, has used satire in an effort to effect reform in his society. His masterpiece "The Rape of the Lock" is generally considered the most popular of his writings as well as the finest satirical poem in the English language. It was written at the suggestion of John Caryll, Pope's friend, ostensibly to heal a family row which resulted when Lord Petre, an acquaintance of Pope, playfully clipped a lock of hair from the head of Arabella Fermor. Because Lord Petre's forwardness had upset the Fermors and the two families had quarrelled, Pope decided to bring them together again. He chose to show that the incident was not a serious one by exaggerating its gravity in a comical way and by so doing made the offended dignity of the Fermors comical too. Pope's larger purpose in writing the poem, however, was to ridicule the social vanity of his day and the importance that was attached to affected manners.

JONATHAN SWIFT

Jonathan Swift has been acclaimed the greatest ironist in English literature and, as a result, has been accused of all the malevolence that resentment can invent. Swift has been said to have hated men but loved individual men. In *Gulliver's Travels* he portrayed his hatred in the caustic political and social satire which he aimed at the English people, representing mankind in general, and the Whigs in particular. It is quite clear to most readers that Gulliver is not really voyaging to different countries, but looking at his own society through distorting lenses. By means of a disarming simplicity of style and careful attention to detail in order to heighten the effect of the narrative, Swift produced one of the outstanding pieces of satire in world literature.

SAMUEL JOHNSON

Samuel Johnson was first known as a satirical poet, modelling himself upon Juvenal. His "Vanity of Human Wishes" was a loose imitation of Juvenal's Tenth Satire. Juvenal's poem and Johnson's are satires in the classical sense and the purpose of satire in the classic view was to reform. The moral purpose of Johnson's "Vanity of Human Wishes" is to reveal some truth, to create in the reader disgust at his own viciousness and perception of the possibility of escaping it. The figure of the Christian hero at the end of his poem is of the greatest importance because it represents the satire's positive standard. Man seems to wallow in vice and folly and his efforts to raise himself above his fellows by wealth or power, scholarship or beauty are doomed to failure. Human existence is chaos but if man is seen under the aspect of eternity, he may have new possibilities and can transcend his limitations.

Although one could hardly call the twentieth century an age of great satire or think of its leading authors as renowned satirists, yet Marcel Proust has been proclaimed the greatest satirist of the twentieth century, and Wyndham Lewis writes of Hemingway, Faulkner, and Eliot as satirists. Lewis considers himself the only writer of fiction dealing in satire of sufficient importance. We may not necessarily admire his satirical efforts or even feel he is representative of our time, but he seems to be within the tradition we have been following.

Lewis devoted his long career to the problems arising from the theory and practice of satire. In 1930 he caused a controversy in the literary circles of London with his satirical novel *Apes of God* in which he ruthlessly attacked wealthy amateur writers. In 1934 he wrote *Men Without Art,* which he claims to have written to provide the theoretical foundations for the great period of imaginative satire which he confidently anticipated in the 1930's. Lewis maintains that satire is a prevalent activity, most people employing it in conversations, and that numerous major writers are to some degree, satirists. In addition to himself, he cites W.H. Auden, a 1930's poet, as one of the promoters of the satirical renaissance, and Roy Campbell, the South African poet, whose *Georgiad* he describes as "a masterpiece of the satiric art." Lewis claims that Campbell's work could compete favourably with any eighteenth-century literary masterpiece.

Lewis' arguments are culled from the conventional stock that has been at the disposal of satirists since Horace. Because of malicious enemies and the nature of the times, controversy is forced upon him and he is finally forced to defend his character against the distortions by writing an apologia. Lewis is ambivalent as to the power of satire to effect change in the world. He claims to have "paralyzed" by the violence of his attacks the most troublesome "Apes" in his neighbourhood, thereby producing the *Apes of God.* The novel conforms to Lewis' proclamation of what satire should be. The main targets are Bloomsbury individuals and types and he maintains that these targets deserve their fate and that the satirist is a public benefactor. He calls himself a "dropper of molten iron" on the victims below.[23]

So far we have been preoccupied with tracing briefly the establishment of verse satire as a literary genre from its early manifestations to date. Some attention has necessarily been paid to its sources and function. Although the word "satire" itself has expanded greatly in meaning, usually at the root of the word is a sense of reference to the urbane mockery of Horace or the lashing denunciation of Juvenal.

NOTES

[1] Ruth Finnegan, *Oral Literature in Africa* (Oxford: Clarendon Press, 1970), 26.

[2] Clement Okafor, "Research Methodology in African Oral Literature," *Okike* 16 (1979): 83.

[3] Robert C. Elliott, preface to *The Power of Satire: Magic, Ritual, Art* (New Jersey: Princeton University Press, 1960), viii - ix.

[4] Gilbert Highet, *The Anatomy of Satire* (Princeton: University Press, 1962), 231.

[5] *Encyclopaedia Britannica*: Macropaedia. 1992 ed.

[6] Sigmund Freud, *Wit and its Relation to the Unconscious*, trans. Abraham Arden Brill (New York, 1916), 148.

[7] M.H. Abrams, *A Glossary of Literary Terms* (New York: Holt, Rinehart and Winston Inc., 1957), 153.

[8] Okot p'Bitek, *Song of Lawino* (Kenya: East African Publishing House, 1966).

[9] Wole Soyinka, *The Lion and the Jewel* (Oxford: Oxford University Press, 1963).

[10] Elliott, 107.

[11] Northrope Frye, *Anatomy of Criticism* (New Jersey: Princeton University Press, 1973), 225.

[12] Edward and Lillian Bloom, "The Satiric Mode of Feeling: A Theory of Intention," *Criticism* Vol. XI, No.2, Wayne State University Press, (1969): 127.

[13] D.I. Nwoga, "The Concept and Practice of Satire Among the Igbo," *The Conch* Vol. III, No.2 (1971): 37.

[14] Alexander Pope as cited in Elliott, 111.

---

[15] Highet, 26.

[16] John Dryden as cited in Highet, 241.

[17] See note 12 above.

[18] Thomas S. Kuhn, *The Structure of Scientific Revolutions*, 2nd ed. (Chicago: Chicago University Press, 1970).

[19] Margaret Masterman, "The Nature of a Paradigm," in *Criticism and the Growth of Knowledge*, eds. Imre Lakatos and Alan Musgrave (Cambridge: Cambridge University Press, 1970), 59.

[20] W.H. Newton-Smith, *The Rationality of Science* (London: Routledge and Kegan Paul, 1981), 103-104.

[21] Frank Magill, *Masterpieces of World Literature* (New York: Harper and Row Publishers, 1960).

[22] John Dryden, "Absalom and Achitophel," *The Oxford Anthology of English Literature*, Frank Kermode and John Hollander, eds. (New York: Oxford University Press, 1973), 1603.

[23] The pieces of information on pages 7-21 were gathered from Elliott, Magil, and Highet.

CHAPTER TWO

REVIEW OF SCHOLARSHIP

A survey of the existing scholarship on African oral literature reveals that a preponderance of the early research on the subject was undertaken by non-African scholars who spared little or no effort in evaluating the quality of the project they had embarked upon. Commenting on the attitude of these critics to their research, Clement Okafor comments that they erroneously assumed that:

> Africa was too primitive to have developed anything of value; hence, anything of value found in the continent - literature, sophisticated political systems, architectural designs or fascinating works of art - was presumed to have been introduced by some alien culture bearers.[1]

A major reason for the misconception is that the majority of the early critics of African oral literature were Europeans and Americans who had to contend with worldviews completely alien to them. Bernth Lindfors in "Critical Approaches to Folklore in African Literature" lends voice to this problem and refers to such critics as:

> Impressionistic critics, whose total contributions to this branch of African literary study consists of offhand remarks unsupported by even the tiniest evidence.[2]

The problems encountered by foreign practitioners in the field of African oral literature are understandably varied but at the top of the list is the problem of lack of knowledge of the African language. One would imagine that mastery of the African language of the subject of study would be mandatory for any meaningful and objective research. One example that never fails to be cited by indigenous African scholars is A.J. Shelton's work, "Relativism, Pragmatism, and Reciprocity in Igbo Proverbs." He states that the purpose of his article is "to penetrate somewhat into collective rural Igbo thought."[3] Shelton's half-baked knowledge of the language invariably does enormous harm. Michael Echeruo's comment on this article is very illuminating because he demonstrates how an outsider's lack of knowledge of an African language can undermine his intentions and cripple his research efforts. For instance, Shelton translates the Igbo proverb "Enwe sị na ya ma ka ya ra wee noo mkpụrụ ụtụ" as meaning "Monkey says that (when) he copulates he eats in order to maintain the seed of his penis."[4] Echeruo explains that the "mkpụrụ ụtụ" is a fruit with a large seed and that most people, particularly children, would think twice before swallowing it since it would ultimately have to be expelled through the anus. This problem is easily overcome by the monkey for definite reasons. Echeruo gives the correct translation as "The monkey said that he knew how big his anus was before swallowing the 'ụtụ' fruit."[5]

Echeruo's observations are directed at Shelton's mistranslation and misunderstanding of the proverbs themselves. He, however, remarks that although the conclusions seem to cohere with the subject matter, they actually bear no relation whatever to the proverb from which they are supposed to derive. He conclusively states that:

> To understand Igbo thought, even to know what Igbo proverbs mean, one has to understand the Igbo language. There is absolutely no other way.[6]

This is not to say that there is no place for the non-African critic of African oral literature or that there have not been many whose efforts have borne rich fruit. On the contrary, several have undertaken, and are still undertaking, difficult, painstaking research "in the field" of African oral literature. The point really is that there are sensitive zones - what Lindfors calls

> The inner sanctuaries and sacred groves - which are closed to strangers and accessible only to those within a society who have grown up learning the passwords.[7]

Chinua Achebe puts it more succinctly in "Where Angels Fear to Tread" where he states that "no man can understand another whose language he does not speak."[8] And by language Achebe does not mean words alone but a man's entire worldview.

In a nutshell, much of the criticism of African oral literature has been far from satisfactory, the reason for this being that the early practitioners of this criticism, mostly Europeans, had failed to realize their obvious limitations. With the current renewed scholarly interest in the area, it is expected that African oral literature will, in the long run, bear rich fruit. The foreign scholar interested in this discipline should endeavour to arm himself with as much cultural information as he can get before attempting to wade into the "arena." By so doing, whether his efforts yield fruit or not, he would at least have been satisfied that he has not had a hand in desecrating someone else's "ancestral grounds."

Nancy Schmidt, another foreign critic of African oral literature, has claimed that African folktales, proverbs, etc., have no artistic or literary merit except "for providing commentary on the actions of the characters."[9] This observation can easily be dismissed as a sweeping generalization. Certainly, one is aware that many African writers, most notably Chinua Achebe, have been known to use proverbs in their works. These works have been proven to compare favourably with literary pieces of similar dimension from other cultures, and in many ways have surpassed them. In fact, other African novelists like Gabriel Okara, Cyprian Ekwensi, Ngugi wa Thiong'o, etc., have used African folktales in their novels, not just for character portrayal but for artistic and literary embellishment.

Thomas Beidelman, also a foreign critic, seems to have depended heavily on assumptions in his analysis of his material in African oral literature. He admits that he begins his

> Analysis of them (the tales) with the assumption that any such popular tale must owe its popularity to the fact that it reflects certain important beliefs and values held by the society.[10]

This kind of assumption can have far-reaching consequences for any researcher because any research based solely on assumptions and speculations would ultimately fail to produce an objective portrayal of the actual experiences of the people being studied. To begin with, folklore need not correlate with values. Some may indeed reflect cultural values, but the same folkloric item may be found in many different and quite dissimilar cultures. Definitely, Beidelman's method of research is not likely to set the pattern for the evaluation of African folktales in general.

Although a large portion of Africa has been affected by the largely impressionistic criticism of the oral literature by foreign critics, the South African situation is different. The white settlers there never showed any interest in learning the languages and cultural histories of the Africans in the region, but suppressed all forms of literature that were meant to enlighten the public about the rich cultural heritage of black South Africans. In fact, the only books that black South Africans were allowed to read were those either written or recommended by the whites. As a result, black South Africans relied only on the superficial accounts given by the whites to learn their oral literature. This situation was confirmed by Credo Mutwa and Mazisi Kunene, both Zulus from South Africa.

Credo Mutwa reaffirms that the superficial critical works produced on the oral literature of his people are due in part to the lack of interest in the linguistic and cultural values of the people by white South Africans.[11] In support of this fact, Mazisi Kunene acknowledges that because white South Africans refused to accept the indigenous people's literary contribution except those produced by whites, the growth of oral literature in his country was badly affected.[12] He further states that black South Africans could not benefit from or participate in the enormous corpus of literary activities that thrived among writers with varying interests in South Africa. According to him, the white settlers repressed literary pieces that did not wholly convey their interest or impression of black South Africans. Consequently, his people were compelled to cope with the distortions and the impressionistic literature of the white settlers. All these, he concludes, contributed to the rather stunted growth of oral literature in South Africa.

REACTION OF CONTEMPORARY CRITICS

The misconception about African oral literature went on until the emergence of a generation of new critics who began calling for a reappraisal of the handling of the criticism of this literature. Some of these advocates for change have already been mentioned: Ruth Finnegan, Bernth Lindfors, Michael Echeruo, Chinua Achebe, Clement Okafor. Ruth Finnegan, of course, has been widely acclaimed as one of the foremost foreign critics who have called for a change in the criticism of African oral literature. Writing on the contributions of the early collectors of African oral literature, Finnegan records that even they recognized that "the texts they recorded could be truly regarded as a type of literature, fundamentally analogous to the written fiction, history, and poetry of European nations."[13] She stresses this point because recent scholars of the subject often give the impression that they are the first to recognize the true nature of the texts as literature. In addition, she records Bleek's statement written in 1864 as one of the earliest and clearest on the subject. Quoting Bleek she writes:

> The fact of such a literary capacity existing among a nation whose mental qualifications it has been usual to estimate at the lowest standard, is of the greatest importance; and that their literary activity . . . has been employed almost in the same direction as that which had been taken by our earliest literature, is in itself of great significance.[14]

Finnegan in an earlier book, *Limba Stories and Story-Telling*, develops a thesis of oral literature as a branch of literature. The book is based on her own fieldwork in Sierra Leone - a meaty collection providing a lavish background of the setting and the society. Throughout her book, she argues that African oral literature should be appraised with the same principles and standards as are applied to written literature.[15] Perhaps Ruth Finnegan can speak somewhat audaciously on this subject, having earned outstanding credentials on the subject and having undertaken difficult, painstaking research in many parts of Africa.

Lindfors, another advocate for change, reminds foreign critics not to "brazenly trespass on territory that belongs to others"[16] without trying to fortify themselves with learning and understanding the people's language. It would appear that Lindfors, himself a foreign critic, realized early enough that that was the only way. Echeruo and Achebe have also stressed the importance of a thorough understanding of African languages by foreign critics in addition to an understanding of the African cultural and social milieu. In his turn, Okafor points out that the bulk of the work done in African oral literature has been that of foreign scholars who erroneously assumed that Africa was incapable of producing anything of value.[17]

Alan Dundes, yet another critic, in *The Study of Folklore*, stresses the need for a change in the theoretical and methodological approach to the criticism of African oral literature.[18] Harold Courlander in *A Treasury of African Folklore* argues that African oral literature can compete favourably with the oral literature of the other cultures of the world.[19] He, like Lindfors, cautions foreign critics to tread cautiously in a territory whose cultural and social background are completely different from their own. Still, on the issue of the call for a change, R.M. Dorson expresses dissatisfaction with the method used by most foreign commentators on African oral literature, especially the proverbs. He firmly recommends that

African proverbs must be studied with groups which use them if we are to understand why so many diverse peoples have been attracted to such sententious inventions.[20]

STATE OF AFRICAN ORAL LITERATURE

A number of critics have discussed the relationship of African traditional literature to modern literature. This question is almost inescapable for commentators on the African literary scene whose handling of traditional literature is usually ill-informed and weighted by emotional considerations. The forces of change, such as the emergence of modern urban life, the spread of Islam and Christianity, and the increased volume of mass communications media may have affected oral literature, but have not eradicated it. In spite of all predictions to the contrary, folklore continues to be viable in both rural and urban Africa.

In his article, "Transition from Oral to Literary Tradition," Emmanuel Obiechina argues that West African writers who enter the European literary tradition still remain faithful to their African heritage because they have continued to use the West African oral tradition. Obiechina specifically mentions West African writers but the spectrum can be widened to include all African writers. The writers' attitude, he notes, marks a reversal from the anti-colonialism of African intellectuals who until the 1960's rejected interest in folklore as the "Africana exotica" of British social anthropologists and European cosmopolites.[21] The change reflects the new African rationalism, characteristic of emerging nation states, and often seeks reinforcement through a presumably indigenous folklore. Those post-colonial African authors who have achieved international respectability and visibility writing in English and French within European literary modes are still truly African because, according to Obiechina, they are simply converting their oral folklore into written literature:

> The essential reality of the contemporary West African culture is that within it, oral tradition continues to exist side by side with the encroaching literary tradition. . . . Whether in the tales of Amos Tutuola, in the novels of Achebe, in the plays of Clark and Soyinka or in the poems by Okigbo, we are aware that the writers are drawing elaborately from West African folklore, traditional symbols and images, and traditional turns of speech, to invest their writing with a truly West African sensibility and flavour.[22]

Michael Crowder in "Tradition and Change in Nigerian Literature" finds it desirable that African writers employ traditional themes to preserve the continuity and vitality of their oral literature.[23] African writers who represent the oral tradition as a major impulse in their writing are therefore being true to the cultural reality.

The point has already been made that some Western commentators pejoratively assumed oral art to be aesthetically inferior to written forms and consequently associated it with illiteracy. Philip A. Noss while undertaking a study of the Gbaya people of Cameroun and the Central African Republic states that:

> African oral traditions. . . have been considered for many years in the Western world as naive tales of grotesque monsters and simplistic accounts of man's origin in a world where his existence appeared indistinguishable from the world of nature that surrounded him. Only relatively recently have Western critics and students generally begun to discover that African tales, although combining the twin functions of entertainment and didacticism, are above all an art form with a full complement of aesthetic standards.[24]

The point here is that traditional African art has been denied the title of "literature" because it happens to be oral, although Noss happily concludes that the subject is fast gaining recognition as an art form. In order to avoid the problems that may be created by terms such as "oral literature," "folk literature," "primitive literature," or "traditional literature," William Bascom has suggested that we adopt the term "verbal art."[25] Attractive though Bascom's proposal may seem, critics need to distinguish between what is African and what is Western in the literature. Traditional African art would generally bring to mind past tribal traditions. Indeed, much of Africa is undergoing a steady cultural change, but still many of those traditions exist today. The terms "oral literature" and "traditional literature" shall be used pragmatically with the understanding that they may refer to artistic efforts that have either taken place in the past or are still current.

CRITICISM OF IGBO SATIRE

We have observed that a generation of new critics has quite recently made some attempt to correct the wrong impression created by the majority of early foreign critics of African oral literature. There is now a need to examine how some scholars have criticized some of the genres of African oral literature. The emphasis here will be on satire, the subject of our investigation. The intention is to find out the extent of their contribution and what still remains to be covered. Satire is a neglected subject in African literary studies, particularly in Igbo literary culture. Yet traditional and oral forms of satirical expression abound in Igboland and, indeed, throughout Africa. We have already examined other general works on satire criticism in the previous chapter. It is expected that an understanding of these works would serve as a guide in determining the proper direction that would be taken in the criticism of Igbo satire. Donatus Nwoga comes readily to mind as one of the pioneer critics who have contributed outstandingly to Igbo satire scholarship.

African attitudes towards satire generally include a greater sense of social function than in Western societies. Functionalism is a key concept of African aesthetics. Although amusement is not ignored, attitudes are defensive about satirical expression: satirists feel a need to justify making fun of others.

One important element in the practice of satire is a general belief in the power of words, and this concept is not exclusive to the Igbo or Africa. But in traditional African satire the belief that words have power is definitely more intense than in Western cultures. The power manifests in a variety of ways. Nwoga in "The Concept and Practice of Satire Among the Igbo" affirms that at some stage in Igbo traditions there was belief in the magical power of satire. He provides this example, from his own area of Igboland, of an old poetess who

> Cursed people with disastrous consequences. One was a man who robbed her of four chickens beside the market where her concubine lives. The man died within two weeks. On another occasion, she was cheated out of a chicken by a family of four men. She called upon the god of their town who asked her to beat the gong and recite curses through the town. Three of the men died. The other went mad and still wanders through the town till today, claiming everybody's property as his own.[26]

Although the relation of satire to the curse in Western satire has been exhaustively treated by Robert C. Elliott in *The Power of Satire: Magic, Ritual, Art,* yet in traditional African satire, the power seems to be associated more with social pressure than with curses. Elliott discussed the belief in the power of the word among various peoples, including the Ashanti. This power seems more a result of social pressure and shame than belief in witchcraft. Nwoga's explanation of the effect of satire among the Igbo could be taken to be the effect on many African societies. He believes that satire should be distinguished from the curse because the curse "calls for some supernatural powers to inflict harm on the victim while satire works directly on the spirit of the victim."[27] He also explains that "the salutary social function of satire is merely a side effect. Central to the concept of satire among the Igbo is the idea of punishment through words."[28] It is important here that one draws a distinction between "punishment" and "reform."

Nwoga again provides examples of African attitudes that illustrate this belief in the power of words on the spirit.

> The seriousness with which satire is taken is some indication of the hurt it can create. On the outside is the modern tendency, common in Africa where words have still so much force, to curb the freedom of the press particularly in matters that have to do with criticism of the persons of the political elite. And indeed, it was difficult for even an educated African overseas to understand how the holders of power in say, Britain, could allow satirical plays and revues on stage and even sometimes attend and applaud. Have they lost all sense of shame?[29]

Continuing, he stated that in the Mbanasa area of Igboland, a ban had been placed on a form of singing and dancing which particularly humiliated girls who got pregnant before marriage, or were promiscuous. As a result of the practice, numerous fights were recorded and this prompted the elders to ban the dance on the premise that it prolonged the punishment. It is important to note that the elders were uncomfortable as a result of the popularity of the songs. The songs had exceeded their traditional context and function and had become less useful and more entertaining.

Satire is believed to have power, and, because of the sense of shame, is used as a means of punishment and social control. Consequently, satire is still used to correct vice in traditional contexts.

In his criticism of Nwoga's views, Romanus Egudu argues that satire among the Igbo has neither supernatural nor magical powers. He makes a distinction between curse, sarcasm and satire, and accuses Nwoga of mistaking spellbinding for satire. He then arrives at the conclusion that:

> Nwoga's notion of affinity between satire and curse, satire and sarcasm, satire and magic, and satire and spell-binding tends to identify them as one and the same thing.[30]

Egudu is vehement on the moral purpose of satire and insists that the aim of satire "is always to expose an offender to shame, or disgrace with a view to making him behave better."[31] He adds that Nwoga failed to merge both the corrective and the punitive aim of satire which would make the victim "change for the better."

Nwoga, in a typescript entitled "Satire in Traditional Igbo Literature: A Reply," refutes Egudu's arguments. He calls attention to the historical nature of his analysis in his article "The Concept and Practice of Satire Among the Igbo" and lays emphasis on the hypothesis that at some stage in Igbo traditions there was belief in the magical power of satire. He emphatically states that at some point in their history "the Igbo did believe that satire could kill a man's spirit."[32] Nwoga insists that the purpose of satire is punitive:

> Whatever the corrective effect of satire in the community, the basic motivating factor to satirical expression is more the desire to attack and punish than to correct.[33]

Following the above assertion, he cites evidence from numerous cultural and literary sources to support his hypothesis.

Commenting on the summary of the views expressed by Nwoga and Egudu, Nnabuenyi Ugonna in "Igbo Satiric Art: A Comment" sees the limits of satirical writing as one of the major points of disagreement between the two critics and asks:

> Is the word-play in the game of draughts satire? Is there satire in "iwa ǫji" (kolanut breaking) ritual or "igǫ ǫfǫ" (religious prayer), and can there be satire in the verbal exchanges between actual or fictional combative groups?[34]

Egugu does not see these acts as satire but Nwoga, on the contrary, sees, at least, elements of satire in them. Ugonna, in an attempt to provide an answer to the conflict, methodically examines the situations. According to him, it is difficult to see satire in "iwa ǫji" or "igǫ ǫfǫ" ritual because the attack is too general to be effective and if anybody is affected, it is not because of satire but because of his conscience. He does, however, add that in a literary setting (in a story or in a play), or when it is intended, breaking of kolanut could encourage satirical expression and gives this example:

> If Okeke has heard reliably that Okorie has conspired to harm him, he could with devastating effect satirize Okorie while breaking kolanut and Okorie would "suffer" through is own "injured awareness of assault."[35]

Ugonna has a similar view for combative situations, including the game of draughts. If the opponents in these situations resort to physical aggression and not to the psychology of words, for instance, their verbal outpourings may not be described as satirical. However, he is quick to add that:

> As soon as they engage in psychological warfare and begin to use propaganda, satire creeps in. The purpose would be to demoralize, ridicule, expose to shame, in order to reduce the resistance of the opponent.[36]

Both Nwoga and Egudu agree that the main purpose of wordplay in combative situations is to weaken the opponent, and finally defeat him. The only point of difference is that Nwoga sees verbal exchanges as satirical whereas Egudu thinks they are spellbinding, and the difference in opinion between these two critics is crucial. In Nwoga's view, there is no significant difference between spellbinding and satire. He sees satire as a kind of spellbinding through the magic of words. To be effective the satirist may employ curse, sarcasm, irony, etc., to expose his victim to ridicule, shame, or hostility; in other words to punish him. Nwoga, therefore, thinks that it is the satirical use of the concept that is the most important.

Egudu, on the other hand, makes an attempt to distinguish between curse (ikpọ iyi), sarcasm (ikọ ọnụ), and satire (igbanye mmadụ n'egwu). He further argues that:

> To satirize . . . means to expose . . . conduct by means of song. Satire in Igbo society is so much a song affair, that it is often done with laughter and apparent lightheartedness. . .[37]

Ugonna observes that Egudu has, by this analysis, tended to limit satire to only "benign" humorous attack - echoing, as it were, the tradition established by Horace. But his illustrative poem "Nwangwu Nwa-Udeze" readily proves that satire is not exclusively benign.[38] Egudu surprisingly breaks up this poem into parts, identifying some lines as satirical, some as sarcastic, and others as curses. This prompts Nwoga to ask this fundamental question in his reply:

> If you can dismantle the lines of a poem and say that this particular line is sarcastic, that satirical, etc., does it make it impossible for the whole poem to be called a satire?[39]

Here, one would agree with Nwoga and Ugonna that the whole poem is satirical, designed to inflict punishment on Nwangwu Nwa-Udeze through exposure to ridicule and shame. The satirical singer carefully employs a number of rhetorical manoeuvres - all legitimate satirical weapons - in order to achieve his end.

Another major argument in the Nwoga-Egudu controversy is whether satire is magical, preternatural, or not. Egudu states that "satire has no supernatural power."[40] Nwoga displays ample documented evidence to support the claim that satire developed from ritual and magic and so has, or at least had, preternatural powers. Elliott, among others, has been referred to as one of the critics who hold the view that satire derives its power from primitive magic. One such type of magic is name magic. This occurs where a diviner magically summons a man's soul by mention of his name and commands it to enter, for instance, into a small animal. The animal is subsequently tortured until it dies. Nwoga further maintains that there is an affinity between some satirical usages and name magic and quotes Talbot's report that:

> Among some Ibo, especially the Ngwa, three or four "doctors" are called in and given presents of kola; these summon the soul of the man, against whom the grudge is borne, to enter into some small creature, such for instance as a lizard, which is then caught, tied up and shot at with arrows, as a result of which he dies.[41]

He then adds that satirical singers do insist on calling the names of their victims. Despite the widespread belief in name magic, one feels that satire is distinct from spellbinding or cursing even though a satirist may use curse or spellbinding to achieve his objective. One would agree with Ugonna that what actually determines satire is the human attitude and the social situation. But Egudu is probably right in his statement that satire does not exist in a situation where two masked dance groups are competing for mastery by hurling magical words at each other, although he agrees they may use irony to achieve their aim.

Nwoga's notion that the effect of satire operates mainly on the basis that the Igbo have a shame culture lends support to the views of Victor Uchendu, whom Nwoga quotes as having observed in a different context that the "major deterrent to crime is not guilt feeling but shame feeling."[42] That is to say that the instrument with which satire wounds or kills its victim is shame rather than guilt. Satire ultimately derives its power from the psychological state of the victim and is generally more effective if the victim displays a propensity to feel shame and guilt.

The function of satire constitutes another area of disagreement between Nwoga and Egudu, Nwoga adamantly insisting that:

> Central to the concept of satire among the Igbo is the idea of punishment through words. It is anger with a person or a group, rather than the sense of offended morality which is the principal urge towards satirical expression. Self-expression rather than communication is the main objective.[43]

Egudu disagrees, stating that "The purpose of satire is always to expose an offender to shame, or disgrace with a view to making him behave better."[44]

One is inclined to agree with Nwoga that the primary aim of satire is to punish the victim through words, but one may disagree with him in saying that anger is the principal motive. The moral purpose of satire notwithstanding, the satirist's fundamental concern is not always with the victim or with moral issues but with himself and his audience. Ugonna rightly explains that the satirist's initial motivation is "first to amuse, satisfy and vindicate himself or his audience and then secondly to correct his victim so that offended morality will be atoned."[45]

But Egudu's insistence on the ethical purpose of satire seems to over-stress the point of correction. In pre-colonial times, satire was a powerful instrument for social control in Igboland and the satirical poet/singer was greatly feared. Donatus Nwoga has rightly observed that among the Igbo, the satirist is viewed with some detachment:

> Though, in most cases, everybody enjoyed the humour and wit of the satirist, particularly where the offence was generally recognized, people who composed the satires were referred to as having "bad mouths." They were kept at a respectful distance tinged with fear.[46]

This reaction is not peculiar to the Igbo; it could be extended to include other African societies as well. Over time, there occurred a slackening of satire's initial power. Nwoga further explains how this came to be:

> Much of the venom has been abstracted from most of its popular uses and more humour introduced. . . . But generally - probably because the society has become more permissive and moral standards have become less certain - satire has become less virulent and people can bear being satirized.[47]

Most Igbo satirical singers are motivated by the aesthetic desire for self expression and entertainment rather than by the ethical desire for reform or preservation of the social order.

Because of the nature of satire, the satirist is not always direct. His deliberate distortion and artful manoeuvring of his material do not immediately suggest reform. Instead they suggest some degree of caution. The idea of caution portrays the dangers that satire entails. Early literary satirists such as Horace, Persius, and Juvenal had to write an "apologia" - a conscious attempt to justify their art and possibly avoid retribution. It was precisely this fear of retribution that prompted Juvenal to declare that he would write only of the dead. The antagonisms that the satirist has faced from early times are enormous. They range from assault, imprisonment, torture, to even execution.

Indirection, a device that satirists frequently resort to, can assume several shapes and it aids the audience to focus attention on the art of criticism rather than on the object of criticism. In the performance of modern Igbo satire, the poet seems more concerned with the audience than with the correction of the satirical culprit. Consequently, the "sins" of the culprit are subject to gross exaggeration and the satirist expects the audience to collapse in derisive laughter at the mention of any of them. The Igbo satirical singer always appears to direct his words at his target while actually focusing his eyes on the audience, from whom he expects admiration and approval.

It would appear that quite often the satirist does not even think of reform, knowing that the satirized is, in most cases, incapable of mending his ways. The motivation for satire in such a situation is to punish the victim and to enjoy a sense of moral superiority. As varied as the motivation for satire apparently seems to be, one can argue, however, that to punish plays a far greater part in the practice of satire than to correct, although in punishing one may possibly correct or deter. This point is aptly captured by Highet who concludes that the purpose of satire is:

> Through laughter and invective, to cure folly and to punish evil; but
> if it does not achieve this purpose, it is content to jeer at folly and to
> expose evil to bitter contempt.[48]

From the foregoing, one can then conclude that satire in Igbo usage derives its power from the psychological state of the victim rather than from any magical or preternatural power inherent in the satirical words. The purpose of Igbo satire is more to punish than to correct.

Although these critics have, in many ways, made insightful and outstanding contributions to Igbo satire scholarship, a lot still needs to be done in many areas of the genre by way of further research. One such area is the oral literary criticism of satire by the folk, the custodians of the genre. The researcher needs to get first-hand information from the native speakers in order to better appreciate and understand how they use their satires. This would inevitably involve observing the people and recording the live performances of the satires. It would also involve observing closely the critical canons that they use, and having to transcribe and translate, and classify and analyze them by incorporating the canons of orthodox literary criticism.

This book is an attempt to undertake this task of observing, recording, and analyzing satirical performances by the Igbo. Since the paradigm is Ihiala, an Igbo town in Anambra State of Nigeria, the next chapter will introduce the people of Ihiala to the reader, their traditions of origin and migration, worldview, cultural attitude, code of conduct, etc., in order to set the pace for a critical analysis of the aesthetics and cultural relevance of their satirical songs.

NOTES

[1] Clement Okafor, "Research Methodology in African Oral Literature," *Okike* 16 (1979): 84.

[2] Bernth Lindfors, "Critical Approaches to Folklore in African Literature," in *African Folklore*, ed. Richard M. Dorson (Bloomington: Indiana University Press, 1972), 227.

[3] Austin J. Shelton, "Relativism, Pragmatism, and Reciprocity in Igbo Proverbs," *The Conch* Vol. III, No. 2 (1971): 46.

[4] M.J.C. Echeruo, "Igbo Thought Through Igbo proverb: A Comment," *The Conch* Vol. III, No. 2 (1971): 49.

[5] Echeruo, 64.

[6] Echeruo, 66.

[7] Echeruo, 224.

[8] Chinua Achebe, "Where Angels Fear to Tread," in *African Writers on African Writing*, ed. G.D. Killam (London: Heinemann, 1973), 7.

[9] Nancy Schmidt, "Nigerian Fiction and African Oral Tradition," *Journal of New African Literature and the Arts*, 5/6 (1968): 10.

[10] Thomas Beidelman, "Further Adventures of Hyena and the Rabbit: The Folktale as a Sociological Model," *Africa* 33 (1963): 62.

[11] Credo Mutwa, *My People* (London: Anthony Blond Ltd., 1969).

[12] Mazisi Kunene, "South African Oral Traditions" in *Aspects of South African Literature*, ed. Christopher Heywood (London: Heinemann, 1976).

[13] Ruth Finnegan, *Oral Literature in Africa* (Oxford: Clarendon Press, 1970), 30.

[14] Finnegan, 31.

[15] Ruth Finnegan, *Limba Stories and Story-Telling* (Oxford: Clarendon Press, 1967).

[16] Lindfors, 224.

[17] Okafor, 85.

[18] Alan Dundes, ed. *The Study of Folklore* (New Jersey: Prentice Hall, 1965).

[19] Harold Courlander, *A Treasury of African Folklore* (New York: Crown Publishers, 1975), 1.

[20] R.M. Dorson, ed. *Folklore and Folklife: An Introduction* (Chicago: The University of Chicago Press, 1972), 119.

[21] E.N. Obiechina, "Transition from Oral to Literary Tradition," *Presence Africaine* 63 (1967): 143.

[22] See note 21 above.

[23] Michael Crowder, "Tradition and Change in Nigerian Literature," *Tri-Quarterly* 5 (1966): 120.

[24] Philip A. Noss, "Description in Gbaya Literary Art," in *African Folklore*, ed. Richard M. Dorson (Bloomington: Indiana University Press, 1972), 73.

[25] William R. Bascom, "Verbal Art," *Journal of American Folklore* 68 (1955).

[26] Nwoga, "The Concept and Practice of Satire Among the Igbo," *The Conch* Vol. III, No. 2 (1971): 33.

[27] Nwoga, 37.

[28] Nwoga, 34.

[29] Nwoga, 36.

[30] R.N. Egudu, "Social Values and Thought in Traditional Literature: The Case of the Igbo Proverb and Poetry," *Nigerian Libraries* Vol. 8, No. 2, (1972): 77.

[31] Egudu, 78.

[32] D.I. Nwoga, "Satire in Traditional Igbo Literature: A Reply," typescript, 5.

[33] Nwoga, 16.

[34] Nnabuenyi Ugonna, "Igbo Satiric Art: A Comment," *Igbo Language and Culture*, eds. Ogbalu and Emenanjo (Ibadan: University Press Ltd., 1982), 66.

[35] Ugonna, 66.

[36] Ugonna, 68.

[37] Egudu, 78.

[38] Egudu, 76.

[39] Nwoga, "Satire in Traditional Igbo Literature: A Reply," 2-3.

[40] See note 38 above.

[41] Nwoga, "The Concept and Practice of Satire Among the Igbo," 35.

[42] Victor Uchendu as cited in D.I. Nwoga, "The Concept and Practice of Satire Among the Igbo," 36.

[43] Nwoga, 34.

[44] See note 37 above.

[45] Ugonna, 76.

[46] See note 27 above.

[47] See note 27 above.

[48] Gilbert Highet, *The Anatomy of Satire* (Princeton: University Press, 1962), 156.

CHAPTER THREE

THE PEOPLE OF IHIALA

Ihiala is a town in Anambra State of Nigeria and is located forty kilometres southeast of Onitsha and twelve kilometres north of Oguta. It lies some six degrees north of the equator and occupies an area of thirteen square kilometres. Its population at the 1963 census was 40,198.[1]

It is bounded on the north by Okija, on the south by Egbu and Uli, on the east by Azia, Mbosi and Ubuluisiuzor, and on the west by the Urasi River and Oru.

PHYSICAL FEATURES

Ihiala is situated on an undulating lowland about 120 metres (c. 400 feet) above sea level. The annual rainfall averages about 152 centimetres (about 60 inches). The vegetation which was rain-forest is gradually becoming grassland. The land is arable and under continual tillage. During the colonial era, J. Watt, a District Commissioner who visited Ihiala from Onitsha in 1908, described the characteristic physical features of the town in the following words:

> Rolling hills rising to a height of 400-600 feet and deep water worn valleys. The towns are built in the belts of forest, but generally the country is open and extensive views are obtainable[2]

The most important waterway is the Urasi River which feeds the

Oguta lake; other waterways and streams are the Omai, the Atamiri and the Akazi from which the Anambra Water Board supplies pipe-borne water to the neighbouring towns.

THE PEOPLE'S OCCUPATION

The most important occupation of the people is subsistence agriculture. Most farmlands are located within the community and families are allocated farmlands from there. Crops are planted on the two-year rotation basis, yams usually alternating with cassava and cocoyams. Farming entails the clearing and burning of the vegetation and the planting of crops. The most common implements are the traditional hoes, matchete, and the wooden digger (mbazu). Fertilizer is sparingly used. During the farming season, many farmers settle at the more fertile riverine Oru because of increasing soil exhaustion. The chief crops are yam, cassava, maize, cocoyam and other vegetables. The bulk of the agricultural production is consumed; only a little surplus is sold. Domestic animals include goats, sheep, pigs, dogs and chickens, which are raised for food or sold. On the whole, these animals, especially dogs and chickens, are very small in size because of the nature of their rearing. They are not confined and fed but left to forage on their own. The most important cash crops are oil palm, raffia palm, coconut palm, kolanut tree, orange tree and banana plants. These are not normally planted in orchards but rather are grown around residences.

Cottage industries include pottery-making, mat-making, production of soap, raffia mats, brooms, ropes, and basket-making. In addition, the riverine villages of Umudara and Akwa engage in fishing, gather rich forest products, and organize extensive hunting expeditions.

THE QUARTERS OF IHIALA

Ihiala comprises ten quarters known as Ebeleri Ihiala. The ten quarters are grouped into two, Ezi and Ihite, each comprising five quarters as follows: Ezi comprises Amamumu, Uzoakwa, Ubahuekwem, Akwa, and Ogboro while Ihite is comprised of Umudara, Umuezeawara, Umuduru, Umuedike, and Amaduru. Ezi is very large, more than five times the size of Ihite. The largest quarters are Amamumu, Uzoakwa, and Ubahuekwem, while the smallest,

Amaduru and Umuedike, are both located southwest of Ihiala. These quarters and their constituent villages claim independent origins.

TRADITIONS OF ORIGIN AND MIGRATIONS

According to oral traditions, most of the quarters and the component villages were of heterogeneous and independent origins.[3] The people of Ihiala do not enjoy a unitary tradition of origin and migration comparable to the claims of some other towns or groups.

From the multifarious traditions one can broadly categorize the inhabitants into two groups, that is, those who claim to be the earliest inhabitants of Ihiala and the later immigrants. The traditions of origin of the first group maintain that these people, who claim to be the earliest inhabitants of Ihiala, have four different ancestors. These are Ara, also known as Dara; Dike, also called Ezeala; Dioha, also called Awala; and Dim Ogboro. It is claimed that these ancestors did not migrate to Ihiala, but had occupied their ancestral homeland from the earliest times. For clarity, it is necessary to discuss these ancestors to show their influence on the social and cultural life of the people.

ARA OR DARA

Tradition has it that Ara, commonly reputed to be the father of Umudara, was in Ihiala from the beginning of creation. As a result of this, he named the area Ala Ara (Ara's land), after himself. Four groups of immigrants later arrived in Ala Ara and Ara gave them land on which they settled. The immigrants were the Amaduru, who came from Orsumoghu; Umuezeawara, who arrived from Ohakpu near Uli; Umuduru-Oru, who came from Mbosi; and Umuedike, who came from Onitsha. Ara extended his political authority over them and gave them the name Ihe Ara Nwere (those owned by Ara). Ara later assigned religious functions to two of the groups and made Umuduru the high priest of Urasi, the oldest and highest deity of Ihiala, while he put Amaduru in charge of Ikenga (the war deity and god of victory). These four villages make up a big subdivision of Ihiala called Ihite with Umudara as the head.

This tradition is widely believed in Ihiala and some internal evidence appears to lend support to its authenticity. Geographically, Umudara is located at a strategic site, at the confluence of the Urasi River and its tributary, Atamiri. Although these rivers appear narrow and shallow today, in those early times they certainly constituted physical barriers and therefore provided natural protection against external attack. Their annual floods, in addition, improved the fertility of the soil, increased fish stock and provided drinking water.

In spite of her small size, Umudara is still the head of the five quarters that constitute Ihite. In the religious sphere Umudara is still the supreme high priest of Ihite; she breaks kolanut for them and also confers ǫzǫ (traditional) titles on all other villages of Ihite quarter. M.G. Smith, in his report of the inquiry into Ihiala chieftaincy dispute, confirms that Umudara's spiritual hegemony extends over all Ihiala in the blessing of the kolanut, and in playing a key part in the installation of the Oluoha, the paramount chief of Ihiala.[4] In an interview, Mbalaso Odimegwu explained that before the British established their rule over Ihiala in about 1910, it was the Eze Dara (High Priest of Dara) who had the sole authority of condemning to death any person who committed certain abominations, such as yam stealing.[5]

DIKE OR EZEALA

Ezeala (chief of the land), nicknamed Dike (strong man) because of his military exploits, was identified as the father of the village of Umudike. Tradition maintains that at first Dike lived at the site which is still known as Ihu ala Dike.

Like the hospitable Dara, Dike permitted some migrant groups to settle with him. These were Meri who fled to Dike from Amamumu and whose descendants today are the Umumeri and Duru, a famous medicine man and the ancestor of the village of Umuduru (Uzoakwa). Duru migrated from Mbosi, a neighbouring town, and Dike made him the high priest of the Ala deity, his spiritual duty being the daily offering of sacrifices to propitiate the gods of Uzoakwa. The third migrant was Mkpume and his young son, and it is believed that both migrated from Onicha Olona and, having crossed the River Niger, eventually reached Ihiala.

At first, Mkpume settled with Dara but when they quarrelled the former was forced to move about six kilometres northwards to settle with Dike. Here Mkpume begot four sons and a daughter from whom descended the villages of Umuezeotutu, Umuarugwu, Umuosobe, Umuokporogbu and Umudubiri. The last migrant who settled with Dike was a war captive named Egorom. Dike captured him in a war across the River Niger and resettled him in his domain.

These settlements for the migrants together with Umudike make up the village group called Ebeteghete Uzoakwa (nine villages of Uzoakwa), with the Okpara (eldest man) of Umudike as its head and high priest.

DIOHA AWALA

Another founding father was Dioha Awala. Very little is known about this ancestor or his descendants but a handful of the surviving descendants can, however, be traced, their total extinction having been prevented by Okohia village. Traditions from some quarters hold that Dioha Awala was in existence from the earliest times having "germinated" from the ground after a deluge had destroyed the first world.[6]

With population growth and perhaps the need for more land, Dioha Awala was soon involved in a bitter war with very powerful enemies who probably came from Ubuluisiuzor and who proved too strong for him. Dioha Awala was therefore forced to enter into military alliance with his contemporaries namely, Dara, Dim Ogboro and Dike, who helped him to subdue the enemies. No sooner had this war ended than Dioha became involved in a more bitter and bloodier war with two neighbouring towns called Uzi and Isiakpu. Dioha escaped defeat by the timely intervention of the great warrior, Dike, who destroyed the opposing forces. Dike annexed the territories formerly inhabited by Uzi and Isiakpu as a reward for his brilliant victory over the enemies. The capture of Uzi and Isiakpu forced all the inhabitants to flee to other parts of Ihiala. Today only a negligible few of the descendants of Uzi and Isiakpu can be traced and these have completely lost their original identity as a group.

To obtain spiritual aid in preventing future attacks on his land, Dioha, through gifts of land and other privileges, enticed two Nri priests named Onyeije and Ukabia, to settle with him. Ukabia later had a son whom he named "Ihu Dioha Awala ji m alala" (Dioha's hospitality has stopped me from returning home (to Nri). This name was later shortened to Ihuejim. In due course, Dioha Awala made Ihuejim the high priest of Aho Ejimoke (the smallpox deity), and gave him significant functions in many ritual ceremonies, especially in Ozo title-taking.

Today, a handful of descendants of Awala can be traced to Umuawa, a tiny lineage within the small village of Umunnebogbu in

Ohohia. Even the eldest of these descendants is unable to account for the sparseness of their population, or to give an account of what happened to their forebears. They presupposed that the Uzi and Isiakpu whom they conquered and dispossessed might have used charms to wipe away their ancestors. Here one may add that other reasons for the decline of the group could be the great loss of life resulting from the three wars mentioned above, and high mortality from smallpox. The people were compelled to erect a sacred shrine for the smallpox deity in atonement. Other reasons could be misfortunes, hostility or even extermination of this group at some phase of its history by later immigrants.

DIM OGBORO

There are three versions of the tradition about the origin of Ogboro. The first holds that Dim Ogboro, the putative ancestor of Ogboro "emerged" from the ground.[7] This version also has it that with time many immigrants from Okporo (about ten kilometres southeast of Ihiala) in the Orlu Local Government Area of Imo State arrived and settled in Ogboro and that the Ogboro eventually assimilated them. Another version maintains that Ogboro was a descendant of an Nri priest named Ara, one of the earliest settlers in Ihiala, and his first abode was at the Ude Urasi Ogboro. The third version, while agreeing that the Ogboro came from Okporo, claims that they arrived after Ihiala had been occupied by the earliest settlers and, as a result, settled on the fringes of Ihiala and then became known as "Ogboro isi ala" (Ogboro that lived on the border).

From these three versions the following salient points stand out. The first is that it is hardly surprising that some people migrated from Okporo in Orlu. G.I. Jones has explained in his book that the Nri-Awka-Orlu complex was the centre of Igbo settlement, a centre from where migrants set out to occupy other parts of Igboland.[8] These migrations from the Igbo heartland did not exactly constitute a mass exodus of, say, a clan; they rather constituted migrations undertaken by little groups at irregular intervals. One of such groups probably reached Ihiala but was absorbed in Ogboro.

Secondly, one could dismiss the third version as unlikely for two reasons. The first is that neither the present nor the original site of Ogboro is on the border, and, secondly, its source is from Umudara with whom Ogboro has had disputes over the traditional rulership of

Ihiala. The first and second versions therefore appear to be more acceptable on the grounds that the first is from an independent and probably impartial source, and the second is from an Ogboro elder who is deemed reliable. It is possible that the connection with Nri may have been invented in an attempt to give their quarter an undue ritual advantage.

Thirdly, internal evidence tends to support the antiquity of Ogboro in Ihiala. Tradition throughout the town maintains that Ogboro was originally a separate town. This view stems from the fact that Ogboro does not keep the same calendar or observe the same festivals with the rest of Ihiala but keeps her own calendar known as Ahọ Ogboro (Ogboro's year). Her festival of Ida Ji (a festival in honour of the yam), for instance, is celebrated on a different date from the rest of the town. Furthermore, she has her own distinct Urasi deity called Urasi Ogboro which is still in existence. Finally, it is important to mention that in the past if a native of Ihiala committed an abomination, like murder, and fled to Ogboro, he was granted political asylum because Ogboro was regarded as another town.

From the foregoing discussion, one can conclude that the Ogboro migrated to Ihiala from Okporo in Orlu, and were probably among the earliest settlers in the town. The claim that Ogboro was autochthonous should be taken with caution especially as all other versions of Ogboro tradition agree that the Ogboro were immigrants.

The population of Ogboro later began to dwindle as a result of deaths through wars and epidemics, especially the occasional outbreaks of cholera and smallpox which claimed many lives. These disasters drastically reduced their population and left them at the mercy of predators. In order to forestall annexation or extinction, Ogboro joined forces with Ihiala and both became one clan.

One might say that available evidence suggests that the claims of the descendants of these four earliest settlers, Umudara, Umudike, Umuawala, and Ogboro, that they have lived in Ihiala from the earliest times, may have some kernel of truth. Again, evidence from quarters such as Akwa and Uzoakwa supports these claims. Some historians are also of the opinion that many Igbo communities have lived in their present settlement from the "dawn of history." Elizabeth Isichei reaffirms that belief in the following words:

> The history of many people begins with a migration, and a founding father. But the available evidence suggests that the Ibo (Igbo) and

their forebears have lived in their present homes from the dawn of history.[9]

Finally, it is necessary to add that even though these traditions are popular at present, there is not yet enough historical (not to mention archaeological) evidence to establish these claims on a firm and incontrovertible foundation.   Although it is possible that the four founding fathers migrated to Ihiala from elsewhere at a time so remote in history that the event has been lost to memory, the migrations of later settlers are still remembered clearly.

THE LATER IMMIGRANTS
AKWA

Tradition has it that the Akwa people were among the earliest immigrants to Ihiala. They were led by a man called Ezikenyi who is popularly believed to have migrated from Egbu, ten kilometres southwest of Ihiala. Having left Egbu, the group first settled at Mbosi, four kilometres northeast of Ihiala, and from there they reached Ihiala. On arrival they settled at Udengwu, one of the territories ruled by Ara. Tradition records that with population explosion and the need for a more fertile land the group abandoned Udengwu and moved to Otoro, and from there to their present littoral site on the Urasi River.

The second version while agreeing that Ezikenyi was the putative ancestor of Akwa accords him Benin ancestry claiming that he and his followers left Ikwume to escape the oppression of the Oba of Benin. They migrated through Igala and Osumenyi where they stayed for a short while. This version maintains that to this day relations of the Akwa still live in Osumenyi. Setting out again from Osumenyi they eventually reached Ihiala and settled at Udengwu, a place not far from "Araland" (Ihiala). From this point the second version agrees with the first, but it goes further to explain that the migration from Udengwu to the present riverine site of Akwa occurred because of conflict between the Akwa and another group of immigrants led by Dioha Ihe.

One may state here that the Benin origin does not stand a critical evaluation owing to a lack of evidence to support the claim. Not much is known about the relationship between Akwa and Osumenyi but it is possible that some members of the group settled in Osumenyi on their way to Ihiala, or that the real centre of migration was Osumenyi. In any case, further research may throw more light on the relationship between Osumenyi and Akwa Ezikenyi as the two names seem to suggest some relationship.

AMAMUMU

The most powerful group of all the immigrants was led by a man named Dioha Ihe. He was the ancestor of most of the villages in Amamumu quarter. Some versions of the tradition hold that Dioha Ihe came from Benin while others claim that he came from Ihembosi, six kilometres northeast of Ihiala.

Those who accord Dioha Benin ancestry claim that he left Benin when he was not allowed to become the Oba of Benin and stopped at Ihembosi from where he eventually reached Ihiala. This Benin origin is fast assuming the "official" version in some parts of Amamumu and Akwa and may contain a kernel of historical truth. After all, some other Igbo groups, such as the Oguta, Onitsha, Agbor, and Ogwashi-Ukwu, to mention just four, have claimed Benin origin and their claims have been validated.

The proponents of the Benin origin base their claim on the fact that Dioha Ihe eventually became Eze (paramount chief) in Ihiala, and currently only descendants of Dioha Ihe can become Oluoha (paramount chief) in Ihiala. This political institution is certainly not enough evidence to accord him Benin ancestry. The present Ezeship does not even remotely resemble Edo kingship and does not embody Edo court, palace or political terminologies. It could be argued that if Dioha Ihe and his group had come from Benin they would have brought to Ihiala some traits of Edo culture, such as language, religion, rituals, and Edo names, and not just kingship institution alone. A critical historian would hesitate to accept the Benin ancestry as there seems to be no corroborating evidence of Benin imprint on the social, political or linguistic structure of the Amamumu and Akwa.

Furthermore, if Dioha Ihe or Dioha Mburuzo (or Ezike Enyi) was a Bini, then his name was foreign to Benin because both names are Igbo names and not Edo names; the surname Ihe appears to be the prefix in Ihembosi. Culturally, too, the pattern of life in Amamumu and Akwa is essentially Igbo. Even if one grants that one or two Edo cultural traits could be found in Amamumu or Akwa, this would still leave the claim to Benin origin far-fetched since groups have been known to borrow freely from one another.

From the discussion so far and bearing in mind Jan Vansina's caution in *Oral Tradition* that " . . . should a tradition contain some internal contradiction . . . it must be regarded as unreliable,"[10] it would be reasonable to look for the origin of the Amamumu and Akwa elsewhere.

Continuing, this version states that Dioha fled from Ihembosi because he killed an opponent in an inter-village fighting between Ihembosi and Ihe-Ehi, a nearby village. Dioha's offence was called Igbu Ochu (murder) which was an abomination in Ogu Okpiri (club fighting) because no townsman should kill another. This crime forced Dioha to flee to Ihiala to escape impending vengeance. It is possible, however, that other reasons such as the search for a better defensive site against enemies, epidemics, famine, or impelling curiosity, might have forced the group to leave under the leadership of Dioha Ihe.

When Dioha and his followers arrived at Ihiala they settled with Dara at Umudara. Not long afterwards, Dara discovered that Dioha was stubborn and ambitious and could dethrone him. Traditions in Amamumu and Umudara agree that Dioha's ambition led to a quarrel between him and his host and Dioha was compelled to move to a new site about seven kilometres away. There he settled with Dim Ogboro at the Ude Ogboro. Here also, Dioha's scheme to undermine the authority of Dim Ogboro led to a quarrel and fighting between the two groups, and Ogboro, the host village, was overpowered in the encounter and driven away from her ancestral home at Ude Ogboro and from her Urasi Ogboro deity.

Meanwhile, Dioha's wife gave birth to four sons, namely, Elekechem, Nnebuogbu, Melike, and Meri. With the exception of Meri who later went to live under the protection of Ezeala Dike at Uzoakwa, the three other sons and their descendants founded the following villages: Umuezeogu, Umuabalike, Umuadobihi, Umumelike, and Umuelekechem.

IMMIGRANTS FROM NRI

As time went on, other groups of immigrants arrived and settled with Dioha in his newly conquered territory around Ude Ogboro and Udengwu from where the Akwa were later driven away. A version of the tradition on the origin of Ogboro has it that the founder of the village came from Nri, but there is no evidence yet to support the claim. There is hardly any doubt that the Umuonyeije migrated from Nri; the Umuonyeije lineage in Umunnamehi occupy the highest office in ritual matters among all the seven Amamumu villages of Umunnamehi, Umudimogo, Umuejimoke, Umuduru-Eziala, Afam, Ihudim, and Umueze. This lineage has the Ọfọ (the staff of authority) from Nri which is given to any Oluoha on his coronation. The Umuonyeije take the title Okpara (eldest man) while the other lineages in the village take the title Ezeloma. The Umuonyeije also claim to have introduced a species of yam called Ji Abịị (Dioscorea odoratissima) into Ihiala and this fact has not been controverted. The name Umuonyeije (children of a traveller) seems to point to immigrants from far away and this far place might be Nri. Lastly, the title-taking system which was believed to have been brought from Nri was the brainchild of the Umuonyeije.

UBAHUEKWEM

The last immigrants to Ihiala were the Ubahuekwem led by a man called Ekwem. They came from Ohakpu near Uli and were nomads. Having temporarily lived in several parts of Amamumu and Uzoakwa, they finally settled at Ubahuekwem.

It seems probable that all these movements might have taken hundreds of years since there is no evidence to indicate some sudden invasions. Geographically, Ihiala is situated on a lowland with very few belts of forest and all these made the clan ideal for free movement in all directions. This free movement ultimately encouraged mutual interaction among the immigrants but may also have exposed them to open hostilities by the earliest settlers.

THE ORIGIN OF THE NAME IHIALA (IHEARA)

There are four versions as to how all these settlers came to adopt the common name Ihiala. The first claims that the name was derived from Ara who is acclaimed to be the earliest settler. Ara named the land Ala Ara (Ara's land) and when other immigrants later settled there he called them Ihe Ara Nwe (those owned by Ara). This was later shortened to Iheara.

Another version claims that the name was derived from two ancestors, Dioha Ihe and Ara. This implies that Iheara was a joint name coined from Ihe and Ara. Both the first and second versions agree that the corruption from Iheara to Ihiala occurred with the advent of the white man. The third version claims that the name was derived from Ihealor, in Alor, from where most Ihiala people came. After these migrants had settled in their new home, they retained the name of their original homeland which was later corrupted to Ihiala.

The fourth version holds that when Dioha came to the area he was so satisfied with the fertility of the land that he decided to settle there permanently "maka ihi ala a" (for the sake of this land), and subsequently the clan came to be known as Ihiala.

A critical analysis of these four versions easily shows that the third and fourth accounts are not strongly supported by historical, linguistic, cultural or ethnographic evidence. The people of Ihiala still call their clan Iheara; it is only the educated elite who sometimes call the clan Ihiala. There is also no evidence that the fertility of the soil has been spectacular. With the possible exception of the riverine areas, the fertility of the land can, at best, be said to be average.

INTER-GROUP RELATIONS

The various quarters of Ihiala were virtually autonomous communities in the earliest period of their existence but in the process of time, social, political and economic links began to develop. The various settlements were later grouped into three large quarters possibly for defensive and administrative purposes. These are: Ihite, Uzoakwa and Amamumu. Ihite was ruled by Dara and comprised five villages; Uzoakwa was ruled by Ezeala Dike and consisted of nine villages; Amamumu was ruled by Dioha Ihe and consisted of eight villages. Each of the quarters was further divided into villages and each village into lineages.

In structure and government each village fits into the organisational structure of a typical Igbo community as documented by such scholars as Adiele Afigbo,[11] Daryll Forde and G.I. Jones.[12] The political organization which these villages began to develop was not different from those of other non-centralized Igbo communities. Although much of the ritual and political power lay in the hands of the elders and titled men, every adult male was entitled to express his opinion in his own village assembly. Political links among the various quarters were at first tenuous but with the passage of time the paramount chief of Amamumu acquired more political power and was able to extend his influence throughout the town. This influence reached its peak in the first three decades of the twentieth century.

BONDS OF UNITY

The most important factor which brought together the virtually autonomous settlements in Ihiala was probably the explosion of population. While the groups came into closer contact with one another, the increased population created the problem of land disputes and there then arose a great need for cooperation among them. In an effort to address this need the people formed various bonds of unity. One such bond was the speaking of a common Igbo dialect; another was the worship of a common religious deity.

There was, for instance, the tutelary deity called Urasi which was regarded as the greatest and most powerful of all the deities in the land and was referred to as Urasi Iheara. She was a river goddess whose abode was in the Urasi River, the largest waterway in Ihiala. She had a vast thickly forested shrine beside the central market, Nkwo Ogbe. To retain her favour, the people made regular sacrificial offerings to her. Her high priests were sacrosanct and acted as intermediaries between her and the community, and on important festivals or funeral ceremonies the titled men usually offered a cow to her. If, however, there was a general catastrophe, say a defeat in battle, prolonged drought, or an outbreak of epidemics such as smallpox, human sacrifice became mandatory.

Besides Urasi, there were about a dozen other lesser deities. These include the Akazi, another powerful river goddess; Uhejioku, the yam goddess; Ala, the earth goddess, and Ikenga, the god of power and war. Each deity endowed its own high priest with special powers. The deity would be consulted at critical times for fortune-telling, magical divination or for the supply of powerful charms. The people regarded these deities with awe and depended on them for protection against, and vengeance on, social deviants such as thieves or murderers.

Another major bond of unity was annual wrestling competition, and wrestlers from all the villages participated in the matches. Venues for the matches rotated from one village to another. At the end of the wrestling competitions, lavish feasting in the host village followed, and this practice generated tremendous social intercourse. Furthermore, it was not uncommon for two or three weak villages to form a wrestling alliance in order to match a stronger village. From this simple alliance, others were formed. All these gave the various settlements the opportunity to strengthen existing ties and develop new relationships.

Other important cultural identities include the common belief in the Supreme Being, Chukwu, the Ọzọ title societies, endogamous marriages, the ubiquitous Mmanwu (masquerade cult), common taboos on stealing and murder and the common ownership of a central market known as Nkwo Ogbe. It is not surprising, however, that in spite of all these integrating forces, intra and inter-group skirmishes did erupt at alarming frequencies.

INTER-GROUP SKIRMISHES

Inter-group skirmishes occurred frequently but they were generally short in duration and easily brought under control. The arrival of a titled man (Nze or Okpara) on the scene, the raising of his ivory trumpet (Ọdụ Nze), or the placing of a fresh palm frond between the warring groups quickly halted the fighting. A peace talk was organized on the spot with the Nze arbitrating; he would listen to both parties, apportion blame accordingly, and make peace.

The usual cause of these skirmishes was land dispute. This is not surprising because as population expanded and people adapted to a more settled life, the previously scattered kin groups began to fill the empty portions of land between them. This brought more and more groups into contact and sometimes conflict. The secondary migration of Akwa from Udengwu and the acquisition of the vacated site by Amamumu is an example. Another is the conflict which led to the exodus of the Ogboro from their former abode to a new site about six kilometres to the west of their former settlement and the occupation of that site by Amamumu. The skirmishes between Amamumu and Ubahuekwem, Umuabalike and Obodoawa, and many others can similarly be attributed to land disputes.

Another major cause of inter-village fighting was kidnapping for slavery. This was the cause of the second Amamumu-Akwa war still remembered in Akwa as Ọgụ Ohumba (war against twenty towns). Twelve Akwa men whom Oluoha Odimegwu invited to a feast were kidnapped by their host Oluoha Odimegwu (1908-1938). This outraged the Akwa and they declared war on Amamumu whose superiority in numbers was counterbalanced by the possession of more sophisticated guns by the Akwa, who obtained them from the neighbouring Oguta. The bitterest and longest of all the wars caused by kidnapping and murder was between Umudike and Umuosobe. In avenging the kidnap of an Umudike man by the Umuosobe, the Umudike killed a titled man of Umuosobe and the latter declared war on Umudike. The allies rebuffed an attack by Umudike by sheer superiority in numbers and claimed victory by invading Umudike. The timely intervention of Oluoha Izuogu Ezike brought peace and reconciled Umudike with the other villages.

EXTERNAL WARS

As demographic pressures mounted, Ihiala people began to have more contact with neighbouring towns such as Mbosi, Azia, Ubuluisiuzor, Okija, and Uli. Conflict over land always ensued, but while some of the external wars waged by the Ihiala were wars of expansion, most others were wars of aggression against weaker neighbors for the purpose of obtaining captives. Some of the major ones include the wars against Ubuluisiuzo, Azia, Uzi/Isiakpu, Amagu, Ibi, Amorka, Mgbidi, Ozara, Mbosi, and Uli. In order to show the nature and consequences of these wars, one of them will be discussed in detail here.

THE IHIALA-ULI WAR (1893-1903)

The Ihiala-Uli war was probably the bloodiest and the last external battle fought by the people of Ihiala. It is presumed to have begun in the last decades of the nineteenth century and lasted for many years. According to P.A. Talbot, this war was suddenly brought to an end by the troops of the West African Frontier Force in 1903.

The war was caused by a land dispute between Ihiala and Uli. Eventually, the Uli were driven over the left bank of the Atamiri river which marks the boundary between Ihiala and Uli. The immediate cause of the war was the execution in Ihiala of an Uli man named Akatabam who was alleged to have poisoned the Ihiala paramount chief, Oluoha Izuogu Ezike. When news of the execution reached Uli, they declared war on Ihiala, a war that would last intermittently for about ten years, from 1893 to 1903.

On the first day of the fight each side suffered one casualty. Meanwhile, Uli fighters bribed an Aro trader (travelling trader) named Igwe Elekwachi who was based in Ihiala to betray Ihiala troops. The Aro man lured some Ihiala strongmen to follow him to Ibi to capture cattle which he told them roamed wild there. To their surprise, he led them into an Uli ambush where they were massacred.

The Ihiala, though much provoked, could not launch an offensive at once because the Uli massacre had deprived their army of most of its commanders and demoralized the troops. In desperation, Ihiala hired Ohafia warriors but their cutlasses were inferior to the guns of the Uli. The failure of this invasion took its toll on the morale of Ihiala forces. Then an Ihiala trader named Iloduba Ezurike suggested inviting white-led troops whom he saw quartered at Abo. Thus the elders of Ihiala seized the opportunity of British hinterland expeditions to ally with the British troops against Uli. These government soldiers were equipped with sophisticated ammunition and when they met the Uli troops using what the Uli called Odajirichi (machine guns), they forced them to flee in disarray. The Uli King, Izulobi, was captured and the town surrendered. This brought the Ihiala-Uli war to an end and also resulted in the extension of British control over Uli.

LOCAL TRADE

Inter-village trade was a big binding force among the villages in Ihiala. G.T. Basden observed that trading was a distinct profession and as such filled up the lives of many Igbo.[13] The big market, Nkwo Ogbe, was held every eight days, and still is. Industrial products were sold in this market; the most common were agricultural products: livestock, poultry, palm oil, fruit and vegetables, some of which were brought from neighbouring towns such as Orsu and Azia. The Aro and Nri brought imported commodities such as salt, textile, ornaments and ritual goods to the market. The Akwa and Nkwerre traded with Ihiala in iron goods and from Oguta came most of the salt, alcoholic beverages and gun powder.

Inter-village trade, however, did not flourish due to poor communication, fear of kidnapping, or other forms of hostility from villages along the routes to the market. Villagers from the riverine Akwa and Umueze had to recruit guards to attend the market. Beautiful girls ran an even greater risk of being kidnapped if they dared go beyond their village unaccompanied by strong men, and so the people resolved that this era of insecurity could not continue indefinitely. Because of its adverse economic consequences, Urasi was said to have issued an order through her high priest that nobody, including foreigners, should be kidnapped, killed, or molested on Nkwo Ogbe day. This intervention by Urasi ensured personal safety, and attendance at the market increased. People from as far away as Orsumuoghu, Azia, Ozubulu, Ihembosi, Lilu and Mbosi began to attend.

Furthermore, the Nkwo Ogbe square, like others in Igboland, was not just an important centre for economic activities alone but was also a centre for communication and social intercourse. Important announcements such as the date for the new yam festival, funeral announcements or parades for newly titled men and their wives took place at Nkwo Ogbe. Safe passage to Nkwo Ogbe improved the economy of Ihiala and engendered social and economic cohesion not only among the indigenous people but also with neighbouring towns. Population pressure, pride of place, and other factors gave rise to the establishment of a number of village markets which were dominated by women who sold agricultural products.

LONG DISTANCE TRADE

Many Ihiala people engaged in long-distance trade in Igboland and this brought them in contact with many distant Igbo groups: Arochukwu, Aro Ndizuogu, Bende, Nkwerre, and the Oru towns of Abo, Oguta, Osomari, Atani, Umunankwo, Akiri, and Ogwuaniocha. The long-distance trade was dominated by the Aro because, according to J.D. Fage, they possessed powerful oracles.[14] Ihiala had no widely respected oracle but, in spite of this, her long-distance traders actively participated in this trade. They usually travelled in the company of Aro masters for security purposes and sometimes, too, they entrusted their merchandise to Aro agents who sold the goods for a commission. Ihiala traders traded mainly in salt, cloth, camwood, bells of assorted sizes, hoes, knives, ritual goods and, after the mid-nineteenth century, palm oil. They also traded in slaves even though that was the preserve of the Oluoha.

SLAVE TRADE

It was the Aro who introduced the slave trade into Ihiala. In order to perpetuate this most lucrative trade, the Aro established settlements in Ihiala as well as a network of slave routes throughout Igboland. The most important of these settlements in Ihiala was the Aro colony of Umuogbulafor. Tradition states that the first Aro who arrived in Ihiala were quartered at the palace of the Oluoha where they entered into a covenant with him and his chiefs and this made for reciprocal protection and promotion of trade. The Ihiala held the Aro in awe and regarded them as ambassadors from the spirit world. Later on more Aro arrived, and through their agents who were scattered through the town, they penetrated every village.

Slaves were obtained through capture in external wars, kidnapping, sale of criminals or those who breached a taboo, pawning as a result of extreme poverty, or outright sale of one's child or wife to satisfy a social need such as taking an Qzọ title. Slave trade was very lucrative and may have been one of the causes of the many external wars fought by Ihiala. Since the Oluoha had a monopoly of this trade, he took delight in increasing the number of taboos to ensure the steady supply of slaves. Consequently, the nineteenth and early twentieth century Oluohas were tremendously influential, powerful and wealthy.

THE BEGINNING OF AN ERA:
THE EMERGENCE OF THE BRITISH

Long before the first British government officials arrived in Ihiala in 1908,[15] Ihiala long-distance traders had been bringing home disturbing stories of aggressive acts and military conquests being perpetrated by the white man in several parts of Igboland. These stories at first made no impact on the elders who could still recall with gratitude how five years earlier their alliance with the troops of the West African Frontier Force had led to the conquest of Uli. With the escalation of military operations and conquests, and the effective occupation of conquered territories by the British, the elders began to ask why the white man refused to leave as he did after the conquest of Uli.

There were rumours that the white man had occupied Awka, Onitsha, Obosi, Nnewi, and Ozubulu, which were not far from Ihiala. Meanwhile, missionaries began to arrive in Ihiala. The first were Anglican missionaries who arrived in 1907 and resided in the compound of one Asoegwu Umeakuka of Mbarakpaka village. They preached the gospel and taught schools.

In June 1908, J. Watt, a District Commissioner from Onitsha, reached Ihiala. The cordial reception accorded the British gave the impression that Ihiala had learnt a lesson from the fate of her neighbours and had succumbed to the new government. The District Commissioner called for support in putting an end to such evil practices as murder and human sacrifices.

When the District Commissioner announced that he would establish a Native Court at the centre of the town, the people were mildly opposed to it and suggested instead an alternative site at the outskirts of the town. This opposition appears to be the only expression of resistance to the establishment of British colonial rule in Ihiala, because the people did not want to harbour in their midst the all-powerful white man. As soon as the District Commissioner left Ihiala, the people resolved to use charms and their deities to keep the British permanently away and hired the most famous medicine man to procure spiritual assistance in their endeavour. It is still believed that it was as a result of these measures that the District Commissioner changed his mind in 1909 and established his court at the outskirts of the town. The courthouse and a rest house were subsequently built on the site through communal forced labor.

The court was opened during next visit of the District Commissioner and warrants were given to six chiefs from Ihiala and to others selected from Okija, Azia, Mbosi, Orsumuoghu, Ihite-Owerri, Ihite Nansa, Lilu, Awo and Iseke, with a Joseph Emodi from Onitsha as the court clerk. With the opening in 1910 of the Native Court, the process of establishing British rule in Ihiala was completed and from then on the corrupt and oppressive rule of the warrant chiefs was inaugurated. The political authority of the traditional rulers was swept aside, and they could exercise only their ritual functions. The corruption and oppression of the disingenuous court clerks and court messengers brought about an attack and arson on the courthouse by Okija troops. The punitive expedition which followed gave the British an opportunity to consolidate their political control over the whole territory.

THE CULTURAL ATTITUDE OF THE PEOPLE OF IHIALA

The people of Ihiala have unique cultural traits which include their basic beliefs, their worldview and their efforts to ensure the continuity of their existence as a people.

THEIR RELIGIOUS BELIEFS

The people view their traditional religion so seriously that it can be said to form the core of their existence. They generally believe in the existence of an all-powerful God called Chukwu who accommodates lower gods. Religion is so central to their society as indeed it is to many other human societies, that the enforcement of religious norms is a form of social control. The goals of a society dictate the types of social control and these invariably seek to nurture and preserve life. Thus, core values are derived from the need to maintain moral and religious cohesion and are embedded in a people's worldview, religious beliefs and practices. Every society's goals demand certain values which the society strives to inculcate in her citizens, restrict them from flouting, punish them when they do, and reward them when they uphold them creditably. Religious rituals serve to direct and regulate the behaviour of members of a society.

The people believe in life hereafter, in their ancestors, and in reincarnation. The concept of deceased ancestors continuing to play an active part in the lives of their descendants is central to the traditional Igbo religious thought. The ancestors served as the link between the material and the spiritual worlds. Geoffrey Parrinder, in his work on African traditional religion, observes:

> The spiritual world is so real and near, its forces intertwining and inspiring the visible world that, . . . man has to reckon with things invisible to mortal sight.[16]

The people of Ihiala believe that the material world is peopled by created beings, animate and inanimate things, and that the spiritual world is the abode of the creator, the lesser gods and ancestral spirits; they understand the relationship between the two worlds. To them, each incarnation in mortal or spiritual form is a cycle, a period of time in which to live and struggle and prepare for the next lifetime. This, however, is not an exclusively Igbo concept because other ethnic groups in Africa rely upon the same view for their understanding of life in the mortal realm.

They believe in three stages of existence, which in keeping with their belief, are contemporaneous. The three stages are - the past (relating to the ancestor or a dead relative living in the spirit world), the present (relating to the living mortal), and the future (relating to the unborn, also living in the spirit world). For them, life essentially comprises these three dimensions - the ancestor, the living, and the unborn - all of which play a crucial role in their understanding of life.

At the same time, the people are clearly aware of the distinction between mortal beings and the ancestral and unborn spirits and recognize that there is a division between the mortal and the spiritual realms. This divide reminds them constantly of man's powerlessness in the mortal state. Oseloka Osadebe reiterates that all three dimensions unite to form one sequence of existence and that to live only on the mortal dimension means to be unable to tap all the resources of power available to man.[17]

Elaborating on the Igbo worldview on existence, Victor Uchendu states that:

> To know how a people view the world around them is to understand how they evaluate life; and a people's evaluation of life, both temporal and non-temporal, provides them with a "charter" of action, a guide to behaviour.[18]

Religion not only suffused the worldview of the people but was used to restrict or deter individuals from flouting core cultural values.

THE PLACE OF SACRIFICE IN THEIR RELIGION

The people of Ihiala recognize at all times the need to solicit the assistance and protection of the Supreme being, the ancestors and the gods, especially when they are faced with difficulty. In fact, before Christianity became widespread, it was routine for every head of a household to bring his family before the family shrine to offer a sacrificial animal such as a cock, to render thanks for favours done to them, and to ask for more favours. The animal was touched on the body of everyone present. Sacrifice is central to the traditional religion of the people of Ihiala and the Igbo as a whole. Francis Cardinal Arinze further elaborates on this view by stating that:

> Sacrifice plays a great part in the religion of the traditional Ibos. It is really the essence of their worship, and the heart of their religion.[19]

Arinze gives four main reasons why the Igbo offer sacrifices. They are:

> To expiate offences, both major and minor, to ward off the wicked molestations of evil spirits, to make their manifold petitions, and to thank the good spirits, and the ancestors, and in general to show

their subjection.[20]

The people strongly believe that whatever they ask of God, the ancestors, or spirits will be granted provided that they have the proper recourse to them. Their offerings range from chicken, kola-nuts, uncooked eggs, and goats, to cattle. The people are quite lavish with sacrificial offerings particularly during the special occasions when they pay homage to all the supernatural forces that influence their existence. Two of these occasions are the festivals that celebrate Ani, the Earth Goddess, the ultimate judge of morality and conduct, and the ancestors. The occasions create a forum for the sharing of a sacrificial meal aimed at strengthening the bond between the people, their ancestors, and the gods.

THE SOCIAL LIFE OF THE PEOPLE

A major characteristic of the people is their propensity to enjoy life abundantly. Any form of "blessing" bestowed on an individual provides an occasion for lavish entertainment. Consequently, every social event enjoys an overwhelming participation by family members, the wider circle of kinsmen, and the community as a whole. Perhaps it is worth mentioning that the family we are talking about here is not just the nuclear family but the larger, extended family. The people believe in togetherness, in sharing their joys and sorrows. The assurance of some degree of assistance in times of need sustains the feeling of oneness.

MARRIAGE

Marriage ceremonies provide occasions for lavish entertainment and social interaction and people look forward to these joyous occasions. This socializing brings families, villages, and towns together in friendship and enhances a harmonious relationship among them. Attendance at marriage ceremonies emphasizes collective solidarity and respect for one of the world's oldest institutions. As an institution, marriage is taken very seriously by the people. Although polygamy is deeply rooted in the culture, it calls for a great deal of discipline on the part of all concerned. There is a popular saying among the people which goes thus: "Ọgọ ọnye bụ chi ya" (One's in-law is his personal god). One's "chi" symbolizes a caring personal god which provides lineage, nurture, protection, guidance and success, but which demands obedience and discipline. This is the sum total of the people's perception of an ideal marriage - a give-and-take alliance.

CHILDREARING

Another occasion which promotes the feeling of communality is the birth of a baby. To the Igbo, children are supreme, and on their children they invest practically everything; children are an Igbo man's insurance policy. Although some Igbo communities are matrilineal, the rest of the Igbo are essentially patrilineal and so favour male offspring. Ihiala communities are largely patrilineal. This is not to say that female children are not appreciated but there is always the concern that they will ultimately marry and leave their natal homes to establish other people's families and, in addition, take on their names. Male children, on the other hand, retain their names, inherit their father's property, and ensure the continuity of the family name.

Among the people and in Igbo culture in general, a woman would be forgiven all her "sins" so long as she produced children. A baby crowns a marital relationship and the moment of giving birth to one is a woman's finest hour. Consequently, the naming ceremony is another occasion that calls for merry-making. Many members of the community, especially the women, come together to sing birth songs and dance and rejoice with their fellow woman and the family. Relatives, friends and well-wishers bring gifts, usually cash, for the baby.

The longing for procreation among the Igbo is given expression in the names their children bear. One can tell something of a man's life by the names of his children. Four of such names are: "Obiajulu," My soul is at peace; "Nwabugwu," A child confers dignity; "Nwakego," A child is greater than wealth; "Ozoemena," May it not happen again. Understandably, the ritual of the naming ceremony which takes place after twenty eight days, is an occasion for joy and merry making.

On the other hand, childless marriages are regarded as abnormal in Ihiala and, I believe, in all of Igboland. Because of the attitude of the society, a great deal of misery seems to attend such marriages. Society has conditioned people to view such marriages as intrinsically ominous, like the prospect of total annihilation.

BURIAL CEREMONIES

Burial ceremonies call for collective participation by family members, the wider circle of kinsmen, and friends. People who are in any way linked to the bereaved family make financial contributions or render other forms of help to ensure the success of the ceremony. In Ihiala, there is a general belief that the dead should be accorded a befitting burial to facilitate their return to the world through reincarnation. Failing to do this, their restlessness in the spirit world will haunt their progeny in the human world.

COMMUNAL LIFE

Communal life is enhanced through group dances, meetings, community projects and age-grade associations. The age-grade, for instance, is a social organizational system utilized for labour mobilization to aid development projects.

The village is a centre for various kinds of activities like festival celebrations, masquerade displays and age-grade meetings. These activities are usually performed in the village square which serves as a recreational centre and as a place for the enactment of many traditional and cultural events. Children sing, romp and play in the moonlight particularly during the dry season. There are social clubs in the form of men's and women's dance groups who perform songs composed by their members in the village square, or during festivals, naming ceremonies, or at funerals. The calendar is crowded with festivities and ceremonies. These occasions provide stimuli for dances, satirical expressions and their performances. At all times, the village is agog with the celebration of one event or the other.

CODE OF CONDUCT FOR THE PEOPLE

In Ihiala, there are rules governing the behaviour of the people and measures of social control to encourage observance of these rules. Everybody knows the norms and sanctions against those who deviate from them. John Beattie's definition of social control is pertinent in this discussion. He postulates that:

> To maintain an orderly system of social relations people have to be
> subjected to some degree of compulsion; they cannot, all the time,

do exactly as they like. For often, self interest may incite behaviour incompatible with the common good, and so it is that in every society some rules, some kind of restraint on people's behaviour, are acknowledged and, on the whole, adhered to.[21]

Ogbu Kalu has rightly pointed out that much of the literature on social control is centred around a discussion on "deviance."[22] The word "deviance" can have several meanings. It is most often used in a moral sense, to refer to an action which is considered to be against societal norms and therefore wrong. But it may also be used in a neutral sense for actions which are merely different. For instance, in a society in which almost every woman marries, a woman who remains single is deviant. Deviance invites the use of force and punishment in civilized societies to prevent moral and social chaos. Traditional societies are not governed by the use of force but by "customs." Cultural norms, together with the formal and informal sanctions for enforcing them, constitute the system of social control in a society. Most people do not want to be considered "non-conforming" by the standards of their communities. Because they want to belong and to be accepted, they conform to the accepted norms of society.

In Ihiala, and indeed in most parts of Igboland, sexual promiscuity is frowned upon. Consequently, sexual offences such as pre-marital pregnancy, abortion, rape, incest, and marital infidelity are taken seriously. Girls are expected to remain chaste until they marry. Any girl who has a child before marriage is considered a disgrace by her family and members of the community. Married women are expected to be faithful to their husbands.

The people of Ihiala have a shame culture. In such a culture if a man's vice becomes known, he will be subjected to criticism, shame, and rejection. Members of a shame culture dread public derision. The shame and ridicule associated with sexual immorality serves as a deterrent to the members of the community and keeps them from committing sexual misdemeanours. The fear of ridicule forewarns prospective offenders.

An individual can bring honour or disgrace to himself or his community according to his behaviour within the context of recognized standards of morality. Consequently, everybody contributes in preserving the values of the community. Therefore, any deviation from the established social norms arouses revulsion and provokes satirical expression.

Satire has remained one of the strongest weapons for ensuring social control in Ihiala. Every serious offence or abomination is handled with the urgency it deserves. Yam stealing and murder, for instance, are generally considered abominations. The offenders invariably take punishment beyond the satirical venom unleashed on them by members of their community. Their sanctions range from performing purificatory sacrifices to outright ostracism. This extreme measure is usually taken to appease the Earth Goddess since the offences are committed on her earth, and that earth sustains life. Offenders would propitiate the Earth Goddess, and the cost of the propitiatory rituals could serve as a deterrent. In Ihiala there is a distinction between offences which are abominable or ritually evil, and those which are practically evil but not detestable. Among abominable offences, some are considered major and others minor, but all abominations evoke purificatory sacrifices.

As a result, most people strive to conform to the accepted mores of the community because of the fear of being satirized and disgraced. The use of satire is not so much to teach the guilty person as to draw attention to the importance of obeying societal norms.

NOTES

---

[1] Census: Divisional Office, Ihiala, File No. GEO/78/Vol.11/15.

[2] J. Watt, National Archieves, Enugu, File No. ONDIST/1/6/4, C 2038/9, 1980: 3.

[3] Anazodo Oti, interview by author, tape recording, Ihiala, 10 October 1988.

[4]
M.G. Smith, "Report of Inquiry Into Ihiala Chieftaincy Dispute," *Official Document, No. 18* (Enugu: Govt. Printer, 1963), 20.

[5]
Mbalaso Odimegwu, conversation with author, Ihiala, 12 October 1988.

[6]
C.O. Izuora, "A Survey of the History of Ihiala From Earliest Times to 1910" (bachelor's thesis, University of Nigeria, 1976) 4.

[7]
Izuora, 6.

[8]
G.I. Jones, *The Trading States of the Oil Rivers* (London: Oxford University Press, 1970), 30.

[9]
Elizabeth Isichei, *The Ibo and the Europeans* (London: Faber and Faber, 1973), 91.

[10]
Jan Vansina, *Oral Tradition*, trans. H.M. Wright (London: Routledge and Kegan Paul, 1965), 4.

[11]
Adiele Afigbo, *The Warrant Chiefs* (London: Longman, 1972).

[12]
Daryll Forde and G.I. Jones, *The Ibo and Ibibio-Speaking Peoples of South-Eastern Nigeria* (London: International African Institute, 1967).

[13]
G.T. Basden, *Among the Ibos of Nigeria* (London: Frank Cass, 1966), 194.

[14]
J.D. Fage, *A History of West Africa* (Cambridge: Cambridge University

Press, 1969), 44.

15
Watt, 1.

16
Geoffrey Parrinder, *African Traditional Religion* (London: Sheldon Press, 1974), 10.

17
Oseloka Osadebe, "The Development of the Igbo Masquerader as a Dramatic Character" (Ph.D. diss., Northwestern University, 1981), 26.

18
Victor Uchendu, *The Igbo of Southeast Nigeria* (Chicago: Holt, Rinehart and Winston Inc., 1965), 11.

19
Francis Arinze, *Sacrifice in Ibo Religion* (Ibadan: Ibadan University Press, 1970) ,111.

20
Arinze, 46.

21
John Beattie, *Other Cultures* (New York: Free Press, 1964), 139.

22
Ogbu Kalu, "Gods as Policemen: Religion and Social Control in Igboland," in *Religious Plurality in Africa*, eds. Jacob K. Olupona and Sulayman S. Nyang (Berlin; New York: Mouton de Gruyter, 1993), 111.

CHAPTER FOUR

METHODOLOGY
METHOD OF DATA COLLECTION

The bulk of this work is based on fieldwork. Data were collected through observation. The data are based on the satirical songs collected by the author during her field trips at Ihiala between 1988 and 1994. The collection of the satires was done with a battery-powered cassette recorder and with notebooks to ensure a faithful recording.

During the fieldwork, the author discovered that almost everybody, young and old, could sing satirical songs and had quite an extensive repertoire of them. In fact, the people freely granted interviews in connection with the subject and were, amazingly, excited about the whole exercise. Therefore, the collection of the songs posed no problem whatsoever, and questions arising from them were duly answered by selected respondents. Since the calendar is usually loaded with festivities that encourage the satirical activity, the author was able to collect relevant data for this study with relative ease.

The author's first priority was to collect background information necessary for the study. The informants interviewed stated that everyone in the community who so desired could sing whichever satires he pleased. Hence, the ability to sing satirical songs in the community is neither restricted on the basis of sex nor on the basis of age. Most informants stated categorically that although there were ideal times for the presentation of satires they would readily sing such satires anytime they wanted to or were compelled to do so.

The clientele of satirical performances varies from one performance to another. For instance, during moonlight-night plays the clientele may comprise young people between the ages of fifteen and twenty five. But during traditional festivals, a satirical performance comprises mature men and women, particularly women and, of course, younger people and children.

After collecting relevant background information, the author planned and embarked on the recording of the satirical performances.

RECORDING OF THE PERFORMANCES

The author was an observer in all the performance sessions that she recorded. All the recordings were done outdoors. However, since there were no inhibitions with regard to the presentation of the satires, the recordings were entirely hitch-free. The author recorded a total of two hundred and fifty songs dealing with a variety of themes and noted the demeanour of the singers/performers. She noted during the recording that the singer did not just sing or chant the songs but acted them, used variations of pitch, and aimed at communicating his message through the stimulation of all the senses.

The singer produced at one level a chant, at another, a drama, and still another, a dance. The audience was thus held spellbound, not only by the meaning of words and their sounds but also by the performance. The audience demonstrated its approval or participation by either imitating the singer's movements or devising appropriate actions related to the meanings of the words. This was accompanied by side discussions of the performance and its theme.

TRANSCRIPTIONS AND TRANSLATION

In transcribing the texts recorded during the field work, the author was guided by Isidore Okpewho's statement that

> As editors of oral texts, we have undertaken a by no means easy responsibility of reconciling two media of cultural expression, and that we owe at least to the culture from which we have taken something, the duty not to violate our charge, but to accord it as much of its integrity as the host culture will allow.[1]

The songs were sung in a diction which was easily understood by those bred in the tradition of Ihiala and their neighbours. While recording the performances, the author observed and still recalls the excitement pervading them. The songs, which were rendered in Igbo (Ihiala dialect), were sorted and categorized under specific and appropriate themes before being translated into English. In translating the recorded text into English the author had allowed herself some measure of freedom in representing what she considered to be the appeal of the texts. Though basically literal versions were presented, it was necessary to pause every now and then to decide, between a number of alternatives, what phrase would be most appropriate for the poetic circumstances of the performance, and to the skill and seriousness which the performer displayed.

Although the author has translated the songs reasonably satisfactorily, she is convinced that it is unrealistic to expect of any translation to evoke in a foreign reader the same response as that of a reader belonging to the culture. This is especially true in the case of satire with its strong cultural resonances.

ANALYSIS OF DATA

In her analysis, the author discussed all the songs dealing with a specific theme together to ensure coherence between all the units of the collection. For instance, all the songs dealing with promiscuity, family disharmony, oppressive husbands, etc., were grouped according to their various themes and discussed under those themes. Each song was preceded by a comment indicating who sang it, what prompted it, and the occasions during which it was sung.

Every informant was asked the effect of satire on the satirized. Almost without exception, all the informants said that the effect was to punish the culprit through ridicule and, consequently, cause him to mend his ways. Questioned further, some of them admitted that some satirical culprits, however, are incapable of change.

The field trips were planned to coincide with the actual occasions which provide the medium for the presentation and performance of the satires. A large number of the satires in the collection were collected extempore.

The survey suggests that satirical composition in Ihiala is a developmental activity. Young children have a limited performance repertoire. But once a satirical song has passed into currency, children sing them to taunt people whom they know to be guilty of the offence that the satire refers to. Teenagers and men contribute reasonably to the satirical activity but married women and their dance groups contribute the bulk of the satires.

As multifarious as the occasions for the presentation of satire are, what emerges from some of these satires is, to some extent, a sense of frustrated confusion arising from the encounter with the West. The cultural attitude of the people of Ihiala has already been discussed in the previous chapter. That is not to say that modernity itself has been rejected. On the contrary, the survey shows that almost everybody in Ihiala has, in some way, adopted the Western culture. The issue is that some of the attitudes and styles which some of the people, especially the youth, have adopted are not exemplary.

It has been widely acknowledged that the Igbo, more than many other Nigerian people, tended to abandon their indigenous culture in favour of the European culture. Adiele Afigbo, commenting on this reckless adoption of an alien culture by the Igbo, states that:

> It was this culture which gave our fathers and those before them their distinctive individuality; that though this culture, like all cultures, had its weak points, it also had its strong points; that while casting aside the weaknesses we can move into the modern world with aspects of that culture in order to retain our separate identity.[2]

This unrestrained longing by the Igbo for things European nearly destroyed all the ancient cultural landmarks in Igbo society.

The traditional women of Ihiala, reacting separately to the abandon with which the people of the community embraced the alien way of life, decided to direct their energies to promoting "Ọdịnana" (custom). The "Ọdịnana" women constitute a force that is hardly challenged. They also constitute a major source of the satirical venom unleashed on erring members of the community. The women seem to share Afigbo's plea that while succumbing to the pressures of a fast-changing world, the people should retain those aspects of their indigenous culture which have provided them with a strong sense of individuality and self-aggrandisement.

Having made this point, the next chapter will focus on the dominant themes of Ihiala satire.

NOTES

1

Isidore Okpewho, "Towards a Faithful Record: On Transcribing and Translating the Oral Narrative Performance," in *The Oral Performance in Africa,* ed. Isidore Okpewho (Ibadan: Spectrum Books Limited, 1990), 111.

2

A.E. Afigbo, "Towards a Cultural Revival Among The Igbo-Speaking Peoples," in Igbo *Language and Culture*, Vol. 2 (Ibadan: University of Ibadan Press Ltd., 1982), 5.

CHAPTER FIVE

PREDOMINANT THEMES OF IHIALA SATIRE

In Ihiala, almost every aspect of human activity can actually provide occasion for satirical expression. Satire is such a prevalent activity that practically every type of poet or singer is engaged in it. It is used essentially to comment on moral and social misdemeanour. However, since it is perhaps impossible to discuss all the situations that provoke satire in Ihiala, this chapter will focus on the occasions that most frequently encourage the performance of the satires. Some of such occasions are: burial ceremonies, traditional festivals, marriage ceremonies and moonlit-night plays.

D. I. Nwoga's assertion in "The Igbo Poet and Satire" is necessary for an understanding of Ihiala satirical practice. According to him,

> Traditional societies make a quick and easy transition from the original creative thoughts which determined behaviour to strict patterns of required behaviour which are then referred to as customs. Harmony between people, and between the people and their world, requires an exact observance of these customs. Failure to follow the practice in any area of life, especially with regard to the moral code, immediately invites satire. . . .[1]

In Ihiala, satire spawns a variety of themes. Some of the themes that frequently recur in the satires are: promiscuity, stealing, family disharmony, abomination and 'modern' wives.

SEXUAL SATIRE

By far the most persistent subject of satirical expression in Ihiala is misdemeanour against sexual morality. Again, Nwoga makes an insightful comment on what may be called the general ambivalence to sexuality in the human psyche.

> Whereas the production of children is the area of creativity in which human beings are closest to divinity, whereas most societies acclaim the act of childbirth as that which most fulfils a woman, the act of sex itself has such an uncertain status in the human imagination that most mythologies posit an asexual birth to the founders of their religions.[2]

The predominance of sexual satire among the people of Ihiala simply suggests that they are uneasy with the sexual act.

The theme of sexual satire enjoys immense variety. But the subject can, for brevity, be reduced into four sub-themes:
1. Girls who have sexual intercourse before marriage.
2. Girls who run after men.
3. Girls who have had an abortion.
4. Old men who seduce young girls.

A full illustration of the variety would possibly require an anthology but a few examples shall be provided. The following is a satire against a young girl who has been discovered to be pregnant before marriage.

Ngee k'asį n'akpọ n'iro
Ihe anyį n'anụ ihea omere eme
Ọbụ onye k'ọkwa tụrụ n'ikpu
Ugwu nwagbọghọ nwere emebisiena
Ihe ọkwụkwọ įza oku oputunwakwara anyį
Nnu na ncha anyį onye jini ha
Nwa asį na adį ime ya onye bụ nna
Nwa asį na amụrụ ihea onye bụ nna
Nne akwọọna aka tiere ọkụkọ akį
Nna akwọọna aka tiere ọkụkọ akį
Anyį ja na akpọzį gį nna j'anụ
Hei, ihe n'eme, hei, ihe n'eme

Ihe ọgọ j'enye anyị akwakwaana anyị
Ji mmiri ọkụ ọgọ akwakwaana anyị
Mgbakụrụ azụ oji ọgọ akwakwaana anyị
Gwa onye mere ihea sị ya n'anyị chọrọ ya
Ihe akpịrị n'eme n'ụwa ebuka
Ọkpụkpụ enoro eno n'atonị n'akpo
Ebughị eme anyị n'asọ emeena
Anyị j'ekwunwakwanị okwu n'ọgbọ
Anyị j'atụnwakwanị ọga n'iro
Ọkwa atụrụna fefuo
Onye ma m'ọbụ obu j'abịanị ọzọ
Obu tụrụ pụọ ụchịcha abata
Ara nị dara ada ọkwa omebisiena
Efere mkwuchi ekpugheena na njọ
Ọmụrụ nwa enweghị nna kwarapụọ
I jeenanị izu nị tọkịrị na mpio.

What do they say
Is causing the confusion out there?
Did what we are hearing really happen?
Who is it that the patridge picked at the vagina?
The pride of a woman has been brought low
Shall we still get our share
Of the bride's presents?[3]
Our salt and soap who has them?
The child that they say is being expected
Who is the father?
The child that they say is born
Who is the father?
The mother has done a futile job
The father has done a futile job
We shall from henceforth
Be calling you 'wife of father'
Hei, things happen, hei, things happen
What an in-law would bring
We have missed
Yam pepper soup that an in-law would provide
We have missed
Smoked, black fish that an in-law would provide
We have missed
Tell whoever did this that we want him
What greed does in this world is great
Bone that is swallowed
Always gets stuck in the throat

The unusual that we have been avoiding
Has happened
Shall we ever speak in public?
Shall we ever feel proud in public?
The partridge has picked and flown away
Who knows whether the cuckoo will be next
The cuckoo picks and goes
The cockroach will come
Those breasts have sagged
They are no more good
The dish has been opened recklessly
She who bears a bastard
Should pack out
You have gone to steal
But got trapped in the hole

In a community where everybody knows everybody else, the specific girl to whom the satire refers is known by everybody. The shame and ridicule associated with sexual immorality need no further emphasis. The song speaks for itself. The degree of degradation of the victim is alarming. Judging from the sentiments expressed in the poem, one gets the impression that not just one individual has been defiled but the entire community. It might be necessary here to point out that in Ihiala, and in Igbo traditional society in general, no word is considered too indecent for satirical expression. Such things as certain parts of the body which in say, Western societies, are mentioned with a reasonable degree of inhibition are called by their proper names without resorting to euphemism.

Here is another satire against a young girl who got pregnant before marriage.

Kwenu Ezeude
Ana m asị Ezeude
Ọbụ ara nị dara ada k'ana ekwu
Chikara, Chikara, ya k'ute jiri kaa
Agbọghọ tụrụ ime ọkwa bịa naba
Ọbụ atụrụ jaana ekwc
Abịa n'ara
Agbọghọ ara gị adagwo
Obunuko osokwara ụnụ bịa
Mgbariaugo osokwara ụnụ bịa
Onyeoma Njeriaku ọnọkwa ụnụ nso

Ka Mgbafor Egenti du nakpuo
Ọbụ mkpọọ gị afa ihe ịja eme
Ara dara ada n'omebigwo
Ara dara ada n'ozugo
Ọkwa nụ ogbe ikpu k'obu aga
Ọkwa ogbe ikpu nwa ịnyanga
Nekwa odogoro ihe nwa oji aga
N'ara gị adago nakpuo
Olomgbo kwobe ekwobe
Olomgbo ayọba ayọba

Everybody shout Ezeude
I am telling Ezeude
Is it those sagged breasts they are talking about?
Chikara, Chikara, that was why the mat got worn
Young girl that is pregnant
Go and get married
If the vagina is not willing
Who will fuck it?
Young girl, your breasts have sagged
Obunuko, did she come with you?
Mgbariaugo, did she come with you?
Lovely one, Njeriaku, is she near you?
Let Mgbafor Egenti also get married
If I call your name
What will you do
Is it the sagged breasts
That you are taking along?
The sagged breasts, they are no more good
The sagged breasts, they are enough
Is it the broad vagina that she is taking along?
Is it the broad vagina of the proud one?
Look at the hollow thing (vagina) she is taking along.
Get married, your breasts have sagged.
Olomgbo kwobe ekwobe
Olomgbo ayoba ayoba

The strategy of the singer is to demean the target by creating a vivid picture of the sagged breasts by the six times repetition of it. The singer implies that the breasts should respectably sag only when a woman becomes pregnant within marriage. Meanwhile, names of other girls who have within that period been victims of the same offence have been mentioned even though songs have been made of them. That goes to show that the punishment for sexual immorality continues to arouse interest until the victim finds a husband.

Most girls who become pregnant before marriage are usually handed over, often without elaborate ceremonies, to much older men who take them on to increase the number of their wives and their farm hands. It is unusual to find a healthy young man who has never been married before going to ask for the hand of such a woman in marriage.

The theme of sexual misconduct can further be illustrated with the next song.

Nwagbọghọ ị na nwa ebe akwa
Ị na nwa ebe akwa
Ị dị n'ụra mgbe ana akụgị bongo
N'ọnụ ikpu

Young girl, are you now crying?
Are you now crying?
Were you asleep
When they were playing bongo music
On the entrance to your vagina.

This song is a satire against a young girl who has indulged in the sexual act with much recklessness but is stricken with terror on discovering that she is pregnant. Bongo music, a popular music at the time of composition of the satire, has a rhythm suggestive of sexual activity - a direct allusion to the abandon with which she indulged in and enjoyed the sexual act. At last, the young girl discovered that the resultant pregnancy was as disastrous as the sexual act was enjoyable. That provoked derisive laughter and scathing comments from her peers.

The humiliation associated with pre-marital pregnancy, as has been demonstrated, is enormous. Consequently, many young girls upon discovering that they are pregnant turn to the more abominable act of having an abortion in order to escape derision. The song below is a satire against a young girl who has had an abortion.

Orima orima orima
Orima ọja ana m ịma nne m o
Orima orima orima
Ime kworo ekwo
K'aja agbara m akwụkwọ

Ime kworo ekwo
K'aja agbara m akwụkwọ
Orima orima orima
Ime kworo ekwo
K'aja agbara m akwụkwọ
Agbọghọ ara dara
Shọpụ ya akpọchiena
Agbọghọ ara dara
Shọpụ ya akpọchiena
Agbọghọ ara dara
Shọpụ ya akpọchiena
Nne m ebenwana ebenwana ebenwana
Na nnakpu abụha ọnwụ
Agbọghọ misi
Na nwa agbọghọ hara ime
Ọbụ ya ka nne ya
J'agbara m akwụkwọ

Orima, orima, orima
Orima, would it prevent me
From remembering my mother?
Orima, orima, orima
The pregnancy that everybody heard about
Is that why they would take me to court
The pregnancy that everybody heard about
Is that why they would take me to court
Orima, orima, orima
The pregnancy that everybody heard about
Is that why they would take me to court
Young girl, whose breasts have sagged
Her shop has closed
Young girl, whose breasts have sagged
Her shop has closed
Young girl, whose breasts have sagged
Her shop has closed
My mother, don't cry, don't cry, don't cry
Getting married is not dying
Young girl, miss, and young girl
Who has had an abortion
Is that why her mother
Would take me to court.

In the song, the girl's mother is understandably aggrieved knowing that her daughter has lost her chances of a respectable marriage. Note the reference to the "sagged breasts" and the tone of finality in "her shop has closed" repeated three times to rub in the stigma that the victim has come to be identified with. The offence evokes pejorative comments - a deliberate effort to wound her pride and slash her self-esteem.

In the next song, the victim of the satire has just had an abortion and the members of the community have joined in deriding her and likening the fairness of her dark skin - a usual symptom of pregnancy - to leprosy which is an abominable disease in the society. The contempt in which the victim is held is evident in this satirical song:

Osi agụgọ bịa nee anya
Ọcha nwa Mgbokwa
Ọcha gha gha gha
Ọcha ya eje egbube ya uri Nkwọ ukwu
Okweha izu nwa uri agbachasịa
Ọbụnwaa ọcha n'ọbụ ekpenta
Ihe hee k'amkwachaa m amụ
Ikpu agbabaghị akụ mbe
Onye uwere kọọ ọkọ
Uru erue danda

He who doubts should come and see
The fairness of Mgbokwa's daughter
It looks awful
Her colour was decorated with indigo
On Nkwo Ukwu day
But in less than a week
The indigo wore off
It is no natural fairness
It is leprosy
Ihe hee[4] let me laugh aloud
There is no hair on her vagina
It is like that of a tortoise
When a dry-skinned person scratches
White ants benefit from the droppings.

Again, the crude analogy between the victim's genitals and the tortoise's is a usual, often effective, weapon of the satirical expression in Ihiala. The comment about dyeing the "fair" body on Mkwo Ukwu - the big market day - when everybody converges at the market square, tells the extent to which she would be disgraced in the full view of everybody. Sometimes, partly because of financial constraints and partly to keep it a secret, many young girls resort to crude methods of terminating their pregnancies. The song below is a satire against a young girl who has used pepper to procure an abortion.

Oji ose aha ime
Nkata ose o jezukwara gị o
A nasụ n'ekwe
Ị ma n'ọbụ agbọghọ n'ahụ

She that uses pepper
To terminate her pregnancy
Will a basket of pepper
Be sufficient for you?
All the drumming and chorusing
Is surely on the woman's body.

Note the reference to the "drumming" which is an obvious exaggeration of the sexual act itself.

It is, however, not uncommon to find that some victims of satire can absorb the pejorative comments and at the same time hurl back more devastating ones at their attackers. In the past, it was normal for young girls to marry men selected for them by their parents. A few, however, would deviate from this norm and marry their dream men even though such gestures were not always favourably regarded. In the short dialogue below, the girl, Mgbeke Ochiagha, rejects the man selected for her but prefers another young man, Ojiaga, for whom she is already expecting a baby. A member of her peer group who is aware of her predicament and who has been known to have had an abortion pokes fun at her saying:

Mgbeke Ochiagha sị na Ojiaga
Ja anụ ya
Ya akwụọrọ ya eriri.

Mgbeke Ochiagha said
That if Ojiaga
Does not marry her
She will commit suicide.

Mgbeke's reply:

Ana m ajụ gị
Ka m bụ omezube
Aha gwene m ime.

I am asking you
Although I am guilty
Of every crime
Have I had an abortion?

This short dialogue reaffirms the extent to which abortion is abhorred in the society and also reaffirms the confidence of the satirical victim in her choice of a marriage partner.

Some of the sexual satires highlight the contrast between the expected norms and the specific behaviour. In Ihiala and among the Igbo, it is abnormal for a young girl to show interest openly in a man regardless of the genuineness of her affection. Whenever this happens, it is misconstrued because it is believed that no decent girl should make overtures to a man. Culturally, the ideal thing is for the man to take the initiative in all matters concerning sex and marriage. Any situation that appears contrary to the established norm creates a fertile ground for the practice of satire. In the song below a young girl is being derided for running after a man.

Oyoyo nwa m o
Oyombi bịa o
Ụnụ afụna ka nwa mara mma
Jiri ụkwụ ya chọje di
Kụrụ ekwe pụba n'obodo
Kpom kpom kpom
Ana m achọ di o
Kpom kpom kpom
Ana m achọ di o
Kpom kpom kpom
Bịanị nụrụ m o
Kpom kpom kpom
Ana m achọ di o
Kpom kpom kpom

Lovely one, my daughter
Lovely one, come
Have you seen
How a beautiful girl

Has gone canvassing for a husband
Beating the gong out in the streets
Kpom kpom kpom
I am looking for a husband
Kpom kpom kpom
I am looking for a husband
Kpom kpom kpom
Come and marry me
Kpom kpom kpom
I am looking for a husband
Kpom kpom kpom

On the other hand, the society frowns at old men who are so promiscuous that they go to great lengths to seduce young girls but not for marriage. In Ihiala, moonlit-night plays are the preserve of young people particularly unmarried ones. It would seem odd to find an elderly person participating in these plays.

The next song is a satire against Obodozie who, despite his age, still goes to moonlit-night plays just to get the girls. In this song, he is inviting the beautiful Eucharia to a feast where "rice" would be served in abundance. This would afford him an opportunity to lure her with gifts and then arrange a sexual encounter. He appears to excel in this game as illustrated in the following satirical song.

Agadi Obodozie
Obodozie oji igwe eje mbele
Honjele
Ukeria ada mma
Ukeria ada mma
Honjele
Bịanụ bịanụ bịanụ o
Bịanụ rie nụ raịsị o
N'anyị n'arọ mmụọ
Honjele
Ukeria ada mma
Ukeria ada mma
Honjele

Old man, Obodozie
Obodozie who rides his bicycle
To moonlight-night plays
Honjele
Eucharia, beautiful girl

Eucharia, beautiful girl
Honjele
Come, come, come
Come and eat rice
We are feasting
Honjele
Eucharia, beautiful girl
Eucharia, beautiful girl
Honjele

From the discussion so far, one is made to understand that in Ihiala sexual promiscuity is not condoned. The community voices its aversion to what it believes to be an indecent act through satirical songs.

STEALING

Another offence that inevitably calls for satirical expression is stealing. Certain offences attract more severe societal disapproval than others. Stealing ranks high among what may be considered criminal offences because it threatens the well being of the members of the community. Satires are inevitably composed against anyone who has been caught stealing to warn prospective offenders about the dangers of violating a norm.

The next satirical victim was caught in the act of stealing a goat. The following song composed against him provoked derisive laughter wherever it was sung.

Onye ekwena nwa ya puta obodo
Okwundu ga eburu ya kpo ya okiri
Onye ekwena nwunye ya puta obodo
Okwundu ga eburu ya kpo ya okiri
Onye ekwena di ya puta obodo
Okwundu ga eburu ya kpo ya okiri
Onye ekwena nne ya puta obodo
Okwundu ga eburu ya kpo ya okiri
Onye ekwena ehi ya puta obodo
Okwundu ga eburu ya kpo ya okiri
Onye ekwena ezi ya puta obodo
Okwundu ga eburu ya kpo ya okiri
Onye ekwena okuko ya puta obodo
Okwundu g'anwuru ya kpo ya okiri

Onye ekwena ikwu ya pụta obodo
Okwundu ga eburu ya kpọ ya okiri
Onye ekwena ibe ya pụta obodo
Okwundu ga eburu ya kpọ ya okiri

Let nobody allow his child to come out
Okwundu will mistake him for a he-goat
Let nobody allow his wife to come out
Okwundu will mistake her for a he-goat
Let nobody allow her husband to come out
Okwundu will mistake him for a he-goat
Let nobody allow his mother to come out
Okwundu will mistake her for a he-goat
Let nobody allow his cattle to come out
Okwundu will mistake it for a he-goat
Let nobody allow his pig to come out
Okwundu will mistake it for a he-goat
Let nobody allow his fowl to come out
Okwundu will mistake it for a he-goat
Let nobody allow his kith to come out
Okwundu will mistake him for a he-goat
Let nobody allow his kin to come out
Okwundu will mistake him for a he-goat

The obvious exaggeration of the act is calculated to punish Okwundu and, possibly, force him to change for the better.

It is not only the erring ones who are usually satirized. Sometimes the satire can be extended to include the victims' parents, friends, and/or relatives. The next poem is a satire against Nwozo who has been a thief from his childhood. His wife, Mgbokwa, does not escape mention; neither do his mother-in-law, Awuchiaku, and his wife's relative Odiokpu. This strategy of mentioning people who have committed no immediate offence bares the community's frustration by Nwozo's inability to change. Members of his community probably know that the satires may never change him (they have made songs of him several times), but they still make a song of him each time he has been caught stealing.

Mgbokwa nta ozu awọ
Mgbokwa nta ozu awọ
Nwozo jebe Onitsha
Mgbokwa atụkwa ya ahịa afụ

Oruo Onitsha ogota ịchafụ gbara fadịm
Mgbe ọja agba egwu
Owere ya mado n'isi ikpu
Odiokpu ụsụ tịntị n'ata ọjị
Awuchiaku agba mmịkpọ n'eri awọ
Gwanị Nwozo ejenwana mbuko ohi ụkwa
Ozuzu ohi ụkwa n'eme ya
Atanị dara n'ọbụ

Little Mgbokwa, dead frog
Little Mgbokwa, dead frog
When Nwozo goes to Onitsha
Mgbokwa will ask him
To buy a half-penny worth of something
When he gets to Onitsha
He buys a head scarf worth a farthing
When she wants to dance
She ties it round her waist
Odiokpu, small bat that chews the iroko tree
Awuchiaku, shrunken cheeks that eat frogs
Tell Nwozo to please stop stealing bread fruit
Stealing bread fruit makes him look
Like a bird that has fallen into a ditch.

Nwozo, like some other victims of satire, is a compulsive offender and may never be able to mend his ways. His community may forever nurse the hope that he could change. The general tendency is for people to try to conform to the accepted mores of their community not necessarily because of the guilt of the misconduct for which they are satirized, but because of the fear of ignominious disgrace for which satire is known. In Nwozo's case, his relatives are derided because they are beneficiaries of the act and are incapable of effecting a change of behaviour in him.

ABOMINATION

It is necessary to focus on some of the actions that are considered abomination in Ihiala. Three of the abominations will be discussed in order of gravity. They are: homicide, incest, and yam stealing. Because of the nature of some offences, Ihiala satire had to be categorized into male and female and archetypal. Satires which denounce major offences are known as male (oke ikpe); those which denounce minor offences are known as female (nwunye ikpe). Archetypal satires are used not necessarily to satirize anybody but to hold the community in check by serving as a reminder.

Abominations are very grave offences and are taken very seriously by the Ihiala community at large.

HOMICIDE

Homicide is an abomination against the earth goddess. In the following illustration, the killer and the killed are descendants of a common ancestor, Eriem. The culprit, generally known in the village as "China," poisoned and killed a family of six. The confusion in the aftermath of the killing may never be adequately described. The young men of the village destroyed China's house and property compelling him to flee. In the olden days, he would be dragged through the village to the evil forest (Ajọ Ọfịa) where he would be left to die.

Today, the influence of Christianity has whittled down this extreme punishment to ostracism. It should be pointed out that in the olden days, all criminal offenders including those who had committed abominations were physically abused in addition to being slashingly satirized.

The following song was composed for China after his compound had been levelled by angry villagers.

> China emena emena
> Ihe nkea bụ arụ
> Eriem riri onwe ha
> China emena emena
> Ana n'ọbụ arụ
> Ihe nkea bụ arụ } three times
> Aka enu ba ya ọnụ
> Aka ana ba ya ọnụ
> Ana atụọna ya
> Onye n'akpansi o
> China emena emena
> Imeena arụ o
> Eriem riri onwe ha
>
> China, don't do, don't do
> This thing is an abomination

Eriem ate one another
China, don't do, don't do
Mother earth, it is an abomination
This thing is an abomination } three times
Let the upper hand enter his mouth
Let the lower hand enter his mouth
The earth has caught up with him
He who gives poison
China, don't do, don't do
You have committed an abomination
Eriem ate one another.

The ritual cleansing was duly performed. Since ostracism is the penalty for the abomination of homicide, the culprit must not be reinstated.

INCEST

Another abomination in Ihiala is incest, the "Big Taboo." The people's reaction to the abominable offence, sometimes extremely severe, underlines the revulsion with which they view incest. This is so because they have been reared to regard incest as an expression of a despicable animality. The prohibition of incest is a near-universal phenomenon. Though the actual extent of the taboo varies, the breach of the taboo offends the ethos of kinship.

In Ihiala communities, incestuous acts invoke the wrath of ancestors, which is extended, by implication, to the spirit yet to be incarnated as future members of the kinship group. Incest among the people of Ihiala is in the category of offences which violate the laws of man and nature. A ritual cleansing must accompany any other verdict prescribed for the offence.

Perhaps incest can be borne today because the culprits are immediately thought to be mad by their kinsmen and their community. Their social estrangement which starts with the uncovering of the abomination lives with them and accompanies them to their graves. The following song is sung by women and children for a victim of incest after the act.

Osondu emeena ekwutegi
Osondu emeena ekwutegi
Mana ofeke amaha ya

Osondu zuru ohi ikpu ụnọ
Osondu zuru ohi ikpu ụnọ
Ị chọjere ngee
N'ikpu nwanne gị
Ihe nkea bụ arụ o

Osondu has done
What could not be uttered
Osondu has done
What could not be uttered
But nonentities do not know it
Osondu stole a vagina at home
What were you looking for
In your sister's vagina?
This thing is an abomination.

Purificatory rites had to be performed immediately. The items to be produced for the ritual include one sheep, nine cocks, nine chicks, nine kolanuts, nine alligator pepper, and nine bottles of alcoholic beverage. All this took its toll on the culprit since he had to borrow a lot of money to meet the requirement for the ritual.

YAM STEALING

Much as stealing is regarded as an awful act, yam stealing is an abomination in Ihiala. The theft of yam particularly if this had not germinated from the soil is a grave offence. The act provokes extreme reactions because it is believed to offend the earth goddess from whose bowels the yam was stolen. The seriousness of this type of abomination is reflected in the following song composed against a woman who was caught in the abominable act of stealing yam.

Kwenu olololo   }
Olololo   } five times
B'anyị ọbụ arụ o
Olololo
O merụrụ ana o
Olololo
Ubaekpe ịbụ onye ohi o
Onye ohi ana atụọna gị o
Ana nwanyị n'ezu ohi ji o
Onye ohi ana atụọna gị o

```
Shout olololo          }
Olololo                } five times
In our land it is an abomination
Olololo
She has desecrated the earth
Olololo
Ubaekpe, you are a thief
Thief, the earth has caught up with you
A land where a woman goes stealing yam
Thief, the earth has caught up with you.
```

The gravity of this abomination is declared by the repetition of "Shout olololo." The essence is to alert the community members and rouse them to appropriate action since everybody is expected to join in condemning the heinous act. In this case, the scene attracted an unusual crowd probably because the offender was a woman. But man or woman, yam stealing is a serious matter. The culprit must purify the earth.

Virtually all the members of the community found an opportunity to hurl invectives at the thief - a way of registering their aversion to the abominable act. All the feelings that ideally would be hidden, all the emotions that normally would be suppressed, suddenly found the place where they could be expressed.

FAMILY DISHARMONY

Another recurrent and persistent theme of the satirical expression is family disharmony. This includes co-wife rivalry, bad mother-in-law/daughter-in-law, lazy/dependent wife, negligent/oppressive husband, etc. This category of satire is necessary because it is a means of re-stating the concept of family relationship in the community. The Igbo man's idea of family relationships has been aptly summed up by Romanus Egudu thus:

> The Igbo man's concept of family life is one of absolute solidarity, cooperation, common destiny and commitment, and love that must be apparent, even if behind this façade of overt love gesture there lurks some rancour or disunity.[5]

The family we are talking about here is not just the nuclear family but the larger, extended family. It is necessary here to point out that polygamy is deeply rooted in Igbo society. As a result, every young woman is obsessed by the notion of getting married since the society despises any woman of a marriageable age who remains unmarried. G.T. Basden affirms that:

> The Igbo woman shrinks from the prospect of being husbandless because she knows only too well the disgrace that is attached to that unfortunate condition. Such a woman is mocked and ridiculed, especially by other women while her own instincts are outraged, causing her to suffer acutely both mentally and physically. Not even in death would her failure be forgiven.[6]

Such is the society's attitude towards women who remain single. It does not matter whether their single status is by choice. The point is that society's dictates must be obeyed.

In the next song, two girls are made satirical targets because their age mates have all got married. The younger girls utilize the opportunity of moonlit-night plays to hurl abuses at them and to remind them of their pitiable condition, a condition which may have been caused by their bad behaviour as a result of which men refused to marry them.

Ozimihe na Ubadinoge
Ngee k'ụnụ no eme
Ụnụ na etorịsị
Ụnụ amaha na nd'otu ụnụ
Anakpuchaana.

Ozimihe and Ubadinoge
What are you waiting for?
Are you still blossoming?
Do you not know
That your mates
Have all got married?

CO-WIFE RIVALRY

Many factors contribute to cause disharmony in polygamous homes. For instance, the man may pay undue attention to the latest wife, who is usually the youngest one, thereby arousing the jealousy of the other wives. Because she is accorded certain privileges at the expense of the other wives she, therefore, becomes a victim of the other wives' jealousy and scorn. The song below is a satire directed at the youngest wife by other co-wives reminding her of the transiency of her position.

Ogeri bịa mbụ
Ebunye ya eze
Okpebe lọya
Mgbe ọnọọrọ ahọ nabọ
A nara ya eze
Nye onye isi
Mgbe ahụ ọmaghaba anya
Aghara abịa n'ụnọ
Etuo ya o ji azụ arị akwa
Onye arụ k'ịbụ

When a wife first arrives
She is given the throne
She plays the lawyer
By the time she has stayed two years
The throne is taken from her
And given to the head wife
Then she looks confused
Confusion enters the house
Then she is hailed
She who climbs the bed with her back[7]
You are an abominable person.

Following this is still a satire against the youngest wife by the other wives. They have obviously ganged up against her and, by using subtle proverbs which are satirical, have reduced the husband's adulation of her to outright mockery.

Adamma Obiekwe
Ọbụ nchịta ede bụ ọkụkọ
Ihe hee ka m kwachaa m amụ
O ji ji agba ụtụtụ
Ji j'agwụ
Ụtụtụ akwakporo

Adamma Obiekwe
Is it the bringing of cocoyam

That is the planting?
Ihe hee let me roar with laughter
She that eats yam for breakfast
Yams will finish
But mornings will stretch to infinity.

Because of the nature of polygamy some co-wives compulsorily gossip and back-bite to the extent that confidences are inevitably betrayed. The general tendency is for every wife to assume that she is in a near-war situation since she is continually attacked by other co-wives satirically, sometimes physically, no matter how hard she tries to avoid clashes with any of them. In some cases, as in the next poem, a co-wife is not only complaining about perennial gossip by another co-wife but also bitterly indicts their common husband, accusing him of taking sides and of ineptitude, since partiality to one wife means the neglect of the other.

Egwu nwunye di bụ egwu nkụkụ ụka
Nkụkụ ụka ya bụ yayanya
Mburu ụkpa jebe ahịa
Ọ yaba m nkụkụ ụka
Dibia ụnọ nụrụ anụ
Ebido nrịa nrịa ọkpa
Nrịa nrịa ọkpa ya bụ nsusu imi
Na okoro dị mma enweha ego
Ma nke nwere ego adịha mma
Ebelebe eje ọgụ ma ya eje ọrụ
Alọbata ọgụ asị na ebelebe egbuona
Na nkụkụ ụka
Ma ya esoha je ọgụ
Ma ya esoha na.

The song of a co-wife is all gossip
Her gossip is "yayanya"[8]
When I carry my basket to the market
She gossips about it
When I starve in my house
She gossips about it
The head of the house that married her
Will start shaking his feet
The shaking of feet amounts to sneering
The handsome young man is not wealthy
But the wealthy one is not handsome

Ebelebe does not go to war
And does not go to work
When they return from war
They say that Ebelebe has killed people
It is all gossip
He neither went to war
Nor did he return.

In another example, a co-wife betrays a confidence reposed on her by another by giving out a confidential piece of information to their husband. The betrayed wife receives a merciless beating from the husband but indignantly reminds him of how disorganized he was when he last sent her home. She boasts that, unlike the last time, if her husband dares ask her to leave she will give impossible conditions for a reconciliation. She sings:

Akụkọ nkọnyere nwunye di m o
K'ọjere kọnyere di m
Di m abata n'egbu m o
Ihe nị mkwuru emeena
O sị kwa m naba   }
A nabara mịa o   }   2ice
Mgbe omere ọbịa nkwukwa   }
Ọbụ ọnịnaa m nara izu n'atọ
Ọbụ ya k'ọna ebere agadụ
Oje ekwe j'eweta mpi nkịta
Ị mara n'oje ekwe mkwute
Oje ekwe j'eweta ahịa ijiji
Ị mara n'oje ekwe mkwute

The story which I told my co-wife
She went and told my husband
My husband came home
And beat me mercilessly
What I predicted has happened
If he asks me to leave   }
I will leave for him   }   2ice
Later he will come for a reconciliation   }
Was it my leaving for eight days
Was that why he was parading everywhere confused?
If he will agree to produce the horn of a dog
You will know that it can be resolved
If he will agree to produce the breast of a fly

You will know that it can be resolved.

Sometimes co-wives can be so envious of one another that they hardly leave any room for a peaceful co-existence. The fortunes of a poor wife can dramatically improve most frequently through a daughter's marriage to a wealthy man. Because of the unhealthy relationship that already exists among co-wives, this happy event invariably provokes jealousy and resentment on the part of the other wives. In the next song, a victim of such a situation complainingly challenges her tormentors.

Ụwa kpọrọba kịm kịm[9]   (twice)
Mgbe nna eri nni adịghị nnu
Akpokwara ha kịm kịm
Ọdi ka m jiri nnu were ribe nni
Ana ha akpọ kịm kịm
Ụwa kpọrọba kịm kịm   (twice)
Mgbe nị nna agba ọtọ
Akpọkwara ha kịm kịm
Ọdị ka m jiri jọọjị gwọrọ ajụ
Ana ha akpọ kịm kịm
Ụwa kpọrọba kịm kịm
Mgbe nna ebu ọnụ n'agagharị
Akpọkwara ha kịm kịm
Ọdị ka m ribere anụ n'azụ
Ana ha akpọ kịm kịm

Let the world be resentful   (twice)
When I was eating without salt
Were they resentful?
But when I started eating with salt
They became resentful
Let the world be resentful   (twice)
When I was going about naked
Were they resentful?
But now that I have expensive wrappers
They became resentful
Let the world be resentful
When I was going about starving
Were they resentful?
But when I started eating meat and fish
They became resentful.

The wives in polygamous homes are not always dependent on their husbands. More often than not, they are meant to cater for themselves and their children without any significant help from their husbands. This requires a great deal of industry on the part of the women. The inability of any wife to cope effectively with this situation invites satire from the other industrious co-wives. The next song is a satire against a dependent wife by an industrious co-wife.

Ogeri gebere di
Orie na ndo ọnwa
Ogeri kpa ume ọrụ
Orie mgbe ojiri gụ ya
Uwa nwanyị bụ oruro
A ja m erobe ụwa m o
Akị gbara peni n' Oso
Egbenu gbara peni n' Oso
Ikpu ada olori hee he
A ja m erobe ụwa m o
O chekwubere di fụghọba ọkụ
Iwe ana egbu ya
Ịgharajam ịgharajam n'ute
Ịgharajam ịgharajam n'ogoburu
Ịgharajam anụ aba ya n'aka
Ịgharajam azụ aba ya n'aka
A jaa m abụdị nwa Uwaegbunam (twice)
Uwaegbunam n'agba ọkpụ rịghịrịghị (twice)

A wife who waits for her husband
Eats at midnight
A woman who is industrious
Eats when she likes
A woman's life is all tenderness
I will think about my life
Palm kernel costs a penny at Oso
Palm oil costs a penny at Oso
Vagina that is never idle hee he[10]
I will think about my life
She who hopes on her husband
As she makes a fire
She will die of anger
Igharajam[11] igharajam on the mat
Igharajam igharajam on the bed
Igharajam no meat enters her hand

Igharajam no fish enters her hand
I will not be Uwaegbunam's daughter   }   2ice
Uwaegbunam shows off.   }

The husband should provide certain basic needs of his family such as food, but it is not always so. Particularly in polygamous homes, the wives do not depend entirely on their husband. Ideally, every wife strives to contribute something to be more comfortable. The above song serves as a warning to those who make no effort whatsoever to ease their burden.

MOTHER-IN-LAW/DAUGHTER-IN-LAW RELATIONSHIP

Another touchy issue in family relationships is the relationship between mothers-in-law and their daughters-in-law. In a few situations, this relationship does blossom into genuine friendship and affection but, generally, the two parties have been known to share an awkward relationship which sometimes borders on animosity. Very often, it is the mother-in-law who is accused of causing a breach of the peace. But there are a few cases where the daughters-in-law are considered high-handed and obviously unkind. The next song illustrates a situation where a wife has been driven home by her husband and her mother-in-law is rejoicing about it. She does not hesitate to make it known that it is only through sending her daughter-in-law home that she could enjoy her son's wealth. Her son could then buy her the white man's "tea," at least. Tea in Igbo culture is foreign and to be able to afford and drink it often is a mark of affluence and an elevation in status in the society.

Nwunye nwa m anaana o
Nwunye nwa m anaana o
E doona m ahụ
Ifụkwara ka mhanwazi
Ipetempe
Ka m ñụnwadịa m tii
Nde oyibo.

My son's wife has gone
My son's wife has gone
I have become refreshed
Don't you see my size?

Ipetempe
At last I can drink tea
The white man's 'tea.'

In another context, there is an obvious breakdown in communication between the mother-in-law and her daughter-in-law. Their relationship has deteriorated to the extent that the two women are not even on talking terms. In this case the daughter-in-law is soliciting a response to her greeting from her mother-in-law while at the same time satirizing the older woman's apparent monopoly of her son. In Igbo culture, and so in Ihiala, to ask a woman to marry her own son invokes pejorative implications which are not entirely divorced from the Oedipus taboo. The song is calculated to inflict punishment since it would set tongues wagging and cause the mother-in-law some discomfort.

Ajọ nne di agbagbukwana m n'emu
Ajọ nne di gị kwe m ekene ọnu
Ma nwa gị nụba gị o
Ajọ nne di agbagbukwana m n'emu
Ajọ nne di gị kwe m ekene ọnu
Ma nwa gị kpọrọ gị o
Ajọ nne di agbagbukwana m n'emu.

Bad mother-in-law
Do not kill me with your sarcasm
Bad mother-in-law
Do respond to a mere greeting
But let your son marry you
Bad mother-in-law
Do not kill me with your sarcasm
Bad mother-in-law
Do respond to a mere greeting
But let your son take you
Bad mother-in-law
Do not kill me with your sarcasm

There are also a few outstanding cases in which it is the mother-in-law who is oppressed. This, again, calls for satire. At the event of death of such a mother-in-law, the women of the community would rain raucous satire on the daughter-in-law. The women may resort to violence, depending on the gravity of the oppression. The incident of

Udeaku and her daughter-in-law, Obioma, is a case in point. Udeaku was advanced in age and Obioma did not get on well with her. One day after a quarrel, Obioma gathered Udeaku, dumped her in a wheel-barrow and deposited her in a rubbish heap. Village women and the wider circle of kinsmen intervened and pronounced Obioma's indiscreet act an abomination. They imposed a heavy fine on Obioma failing which she will face total ostracism.

Meanwhile, Udeaku died, and to crown it all Obioma and her husband wrapped her up and dumped her in the same wheel-barrow to take her to the mortuary. At the hospital gate, the gatemen inquired what was in the wheel-barrow and to their greatest dismay, they were told it was a corpse - their mother's corpse.

On the day Udeaku's body was to be removed from the mortuary for burial, the women of the community insisted that her daughter-in-law, Obioma, be taken around in a wheel-barrow. She and her husband again paid heavy fines. The women pounced on their property and destroyed their house. Meanwhile, the women wondered aloud what an effeminate man Obioma's husband was. In fact, Obioma (Humble of heart) was renamed Obiojoo (Wicked at heart) in the satires. There was so much confusion during Udeaku's funeral that Obioma was forced to flee while the women gleefully chanted:

Obioma onye arʉ o
I ja azanwakwa Obiojoo
Onye arʉ o
Ogbu nne di ya o
Onye arʉ o
I ja azanwakwa Obiojoo
Onye arʉ o

Obioma, the abominable one
Will you answer the wicked one
The abominable one
She who kills her mother-in-law
The abominable one
Will you answer the wicked one
The abominable one.

While some of the women were chanting the above, another group of women burst into the arena demanding that Obioma be wheeled around in a wheel-barrow in the full view of everybody. But Obioma had escaped.

In another funeral situation, a mother-in-law was said to have been neglected by her daughters-in-law who were brutal to her and often ganged up against her. The mother-in-law was alleged to have died as a result of injuries she sustained during a fight with one of her daughters-in-law. The song below is a satire sung for her two daughters-in-law during her funeral.

Akwa amaha ama ebe
Akwa amaha ama ebe
Onye awọwuru na nni
Ọ bụ ya ka amaha ama ebe
Onye akwayịrị n'ọkụ
K'amaha ama ebe
Onye awọwuru n'anụ
K'amaha ama ebe
Onye enewuru n'anya
K'amaha ama ebe
Onye e tiwuru n'aka
K'amaha ama ebe
Onye azọwuru n'ụkwụ
K'amaha ama ebe
A kpọha n'ikwu anụha ya
Akpọha n'ibe anụha ya
Ehee ehee
Anyị ajaha ekwe ya.

They are shedding crocodile tears
They are shedding crocodile tears
She that was starved of food
Is she the one
They are shedding crocodile tears for?
She that was pushed into a fire
They are shedding crocodile tears for
She that was starved of meat
They are shedding crocodile tears for
She that was neglected
They are shedding crocodile tears for
She that was beaten to death
They are shedding crocodile tears for
She that was trodden to death
They are shedding crocodile tears for
They think that the kith did not hear of it

They think that the kin did not hear of it
Ehee ehee
We shall not take it.

LAZY HUSBANDS

Another factor that contributes to family disharmony is lack of cooperation and laziness on the part of the husband. Marriage, as an institution, cannot thrive unless there is commitment and cooperation on the part of the people concerned. Since the man is regarded as the head of the family, the onus of providing for his household rests with him. Failure to carry out this responsibility successfully invites pejorative remarks from the wife and the community at large. The next song is a satire by a frustrated wife against her lazy husband.

Adị mma ụtara a dị mma igbugbu
Eji ume eji obi
Nde mụ anya e ribeha
Oteta ụra bụba ụtara
Ogburu ebube n'ụnọ akwa
Ndieme ọha ndieme anyị
Ọ mara mma nkwa agbaghị agba
Okeọkpa kwaara nde je ọrụ
Di nwanyị

Good for nothing
He that has no stamina
Those who are awake have not yet eaten
But he wakes from sleep
And scrambles for foo-foo.
He that has an imposing personality
But has no worth whatsoever
He that looks good for a dance
But cannot dance
The cock has crowed
For those going to the farm
Good for nothing.

The next song for our consideration is a satire by a wife against her husband whom she accuses of undue exploitation of her. She is complaining that her husband lures her to himself whenever she is financially buoyant but as soon as she runs out of money he treats her meanly. The reference to "goat" has a strong connotation of stupidity in Igbo usage. The implication of this is that her husband simply does not regard her as intelligent. The wife, however, defiantly awaits another opportunity for such an exploitation to prove to her husband that she is intelligent.

Di m n'akpọ m nwanyị mma
Mgbe ọ fụrụ m ego n'aka
Ọ kpọọ m ejighị atọ
M bụrụ anụba akụ agwụ
Ọdika ego kọrọ m
Di m akpọọ m eghu
Di m kpọrọ m eghu
Eghu jata aza ya oku ma orue
Di m kpọrọ m eghu.

My husband calls me the good one
When he sees money in my hand
He calls me "most beloved"
I become she whose bride price drains the purse
But when I did not have money
My husband called me a goat
My husband called me a goat
A goat will come to his rescue when the time comes.
My husband called me a goat.

NEGLIGENT AND OPPRESSIVE HUSBANDS

Perhaps another medium that always clamours for the satirical expression within the family is the oppression and total neglect of a wife by her husband especially when she has given birth to children. Although industrious wives are assets to their husbands and families and are usually appreciated, yet the onus of providing a means of livelihood for the family rests with the husband.

Very often, as a result of the size of the family, one partner cannot cope with the demands of raising a family. Whenever a partner does not contribute something to the family, he/she is usually a target for the satirical expression but it is worse when it is the man who has failed in his primary duty. Such a man is never regarded highly by the community and his wife is always pitied. When such a woman dies, her relations and the women of the community make raucous songs of the improvident and callous husband. The song below is an example.

Okorobịa sọọ, dibịa ụnọ sọọ
O yirihaa afe dibịa ụnọ agwụ
Ọ tụbahaa y'ime ihe o ji agwụ
Ji adịha n'ụnọ ma ede adịha ya
Ite bụ ngịga tọwara chakoo
Anụ adịha ya m'azụ adịha ya
Ede adịha na nkwu, ji adịha n'ọba
Agụụ gburunị nwanyị ọ n'anụ
Soronị m jụọ nwoke a ajụjụ
Ọ ja azakpụnị anyị ajụjụ
Ọ bụ agụụ gburu k'ọbụ ọnwụ gburu ya
Ọ ha nọ ngaa sonị m neta
Nwunye di anyị gbakwa ọtọ ana
Jeenị nga o dine were anya nene.

Young man, head of household
Once he is clothed
His leadership is over
Once he impregnates her
He has nothing more to offer
There is no yam in the house
There is no cocoyam
Her meat box is pityingly empty
There is no meat in it and no fish in it
There is no yam in the barn
There is no cocoyam
Hunger killed the wife he is marrying
Join me in asking him a question
He must answer our question
Was it hunger or death that killed her?
People present here find out with me
Our co-wife has departed naked
Go where she is lying
And see with your eyes.

To further illustrate the theme of the negligent and oppressive husband, we shall examine a song in which a man is satirized for not mourning his first wife, Egoigwe, whose body is in the mortuary awaiting burial. Instead, he accompanied his young wife, the "beloved" one, to a ceremony and this gesture was considered by the women of the community as a show of indecency and defiance of the

dead.   At his wife's funeral, the women of the community unleashed
their fury in a satirical song.

Egoigwe jebere macharị
Onyeka ejebe ikpughe ikpu
Ihe nkea ọ na atụkwa ụnụ egwu
Hei o nwoke nkea
Sọrọ ajọ madụ asọrọ
Agbanabara ajọ mụọ ọsọ
Nde ajọ madụ egbue
Onyeka oyiri m o
N'emebisi ana agagharị
Agbanabara ajọ mụọ ọsọ   }   chorus
Nde ajọ madụ egbue   }
Ajọ madụ ọfọ ka m jiri gị o
Ọ na emebisi ana agagharị
Agbanabara ajọ mụọ ọsọ
Nde ajọ madụ egbue
Onyeka n'akpọ ana ngụ agagharị
Agbanabara ajọ mụọ ọsọ
Nde ajọ madụ egbue.

Egoigwe went to the mortuary
Onyeka went to open the vagina
Does this thing not terrify you?
Hei, this type of man
Just fear a devilish person
In running from evil spirits   }   chorus
Evil people will strike   }
Onyeka, he looks like me
But desecrates the land right through
In running from evil spirits
Evil people will strike
Evil man, I am guiltless
He desecrates the land right through
In running from evil spirits
Evil people will strike
Onyeka does havoc all round
In running from evil spirits
Evil people will strike.

The women were unmerciful in their attack of Onyeka and
continued to portray him in bad light.   They accused him of not only

neglecting and oppressing his wife but also extending the same attitude to his son with whom, they testified, he was unnecessarily high-handed. This is unusual because in Ihiala male children are considered "precious" largely because of the attitude of the society. Male children generally inherit their father's property and this fact has contributed in making Onyeka's extortion of a monthly rent from his son seem ridiculous. The women would not ignore this fact.

> A kpọ m na Onyeka a bụ ezigbo madụ
> N'amaha m na Onyeka
> N'ebe akwa ego
> Onyeka rebere nwa ya ana obi
> Nwa ya biri n'ụnọ
> Ọ na akwụ ụgwọ ụnọ
> Ihe ahụ ọna atụkwa ụnụ egwu
> Ihee o ihe nkea

> I thought that Onyeka was a good man
> But I did not know
> That Onyeka was a miser
> Onyeka sold land to his son
> His son lives in his house
> And pays rent to him
> Does that not terrify you?
> Ihee o this type of thing.

The women extended the satire to the younger wife whom Onyeka accompanied to a social ceremony. She had been repeatedly accused of joining hands with her husband to maltreat the late wife. By their chant the women were saying that both she and her husband ought to be at peace since their common obstacle had been removed.

> Efe erona onye ọbụna
> Efe erona onye ọbụna
> Nwoke nwe ụnọ
> Nwanyị nwe ụnọ
> Efe erona onye ọbụna
> Nwa Abazu neehu di nụrụba
> Efe erona nwa Abazu

> Everybody is now at ease
> Everybody is now at ease

The man of the house
The woman of the house
Everybody is now at ease
Daughter of Abazu, take the man and marry him
Abazu's daughter is now at ease.

The deceased woman's relations, obviously in no mood for any verbal exchange, used a satirical proverb to tell Onyeka what they thought of him, as exemplified by the following satire rendered in a subtle proverb.

Kama ọgọ mmere j'egbu m
O gbuo onye mmeere
O gbucha ya ka ọkụkọ
Oke aghụọ ya anya

Rather than be killed by my benevolence
Let it kill my benefactor
After killing him like a chicken
A rat will pluck out his eyes.

The next song is yet another example on the theme of the oppressive husband. In this case, four out of his five wives had died and he is reputed to be notoriously hard on them. Whenever his wives ask him for a piece of land for cultivation, he refuses and asks them whether they brought any piece of land with them when they came to his house. The death of his first wife, who has borne the brunt of his maltreatment and callousness, provides an occasion for the community to share in the general satirical mirth at his selfishness, as exhibited in the following song.

Okereke onye arụrụala
Obiena taa
Kpara nkwụ gị
Kpara ụkwa gị
Obiena taa
Kpara ji gị
Kpara ede gị
Obiena taa
O buru ana bịa ngaa
Obiena taa

Okereke, the mischievous one
It has ended today
Take your palm tree
Take your bread fruit tree
It has ended today
Take your yam
Take your cocoyam
It has ended today
Did she bring land with her?
It has ended today.

THE OPPRESSIVE FOSTER-MOTHER

Another cause of family disharmony is the theme of the oppressive foster-mother. In Igboland, all the women married into a family are expected to show love and kindness to all the children in the household. As a result, a child is said to belong not only to his parents but to the whole community. It is therefore mandatory that every wife of the family should play the role expected of her and satisfy the expectations of all the other members. Below is a song against the oppressive foster-mother by the child-protagonist. The passage is rendered without the chorus which is one expression "Ayoro" repeated after every line of the song.

Nne nne nne
Nwunye nna m o
Sichara nni
Buru nke munwa bu ogbenye
Donye ya n'uko
Nwogbenye tia ukwu ya tia aka ya
Aka eru n'uko
M kpoo nne m kpoo nna m odighi nke zara m
A na m eme ihe oma obu ka nne m puta

Mother, mother, mother
The wife of my father
Finished her cooking
Took mine, the poor one's own
And put it up on the uko[12]
The orphan stretched his legs and his hands
But his hands did not get there
I called my mother, called my father

But none of them answered me
Am I doing a good turn
So that my mother will appear?

When a foster-mother abuses her role as a mother by her display
of partiality, she becomes an object of satire. The society often
condemns such a woman morally but hardly does anything practical to
save the situation for the oppressed child.

Occasionally the reverse may be the case and the foster-mother
becomes the victim of the oppression. One such case concerns the
orphan, a cripple, who vehemently refuses to help his foster-mother
with the domestic chores while over-dramatizing his condition. He
readily solicits sympathy for his condition and exemption from
domestic chores but anxiously awaits his share of the food cooked by
his foster-mother. This, again, calls for satire.

Nwangwọrọ jee gụta ọkụ
Ụkwụ adịha m
Aka adịha m
A ja m esi añaa
Weeburu ụkwụ ja adị m
Jenụ igụta ọkụ
Onye n'asị mụ jee gụta ọkụ
Ọbụ ebere emedị a ya
Gwaya na mụ ajaha ejeni
Nwangwọrọ bịa rie nni
Ọbụ onye akpọrọ oku asị y'ejena
Ka m gwọrọ nụ ngwọrọ n'ụkwụ
M ji eje ije
A sị m n'ọnụ adịha m nkọ
N'aja m eje iri y'eri

Cripple, go and make a fire
I have no leg, I have no hand
How can I as a cripple
Go and make a fire?
She who expects me to make a fire
Does she not have pity?
Tell her that I cannot go
Cripple, come and eat
If I am called
Should I not answer?
Although I am crippled

Did I say that my mouth is not sharp
I am going to eat it.

QUARRELSOME WIVES

In some cases, as a result of individual idiosyncracies, some wives find it difficult to maintain a harmonious co-existence with other co-wives and members of the family, sometimes with the larger community. The Igbo believe that even if there exists some rancour among members of a family, efforts should be made to maintain the bond of unity and understanding, and not give outsiders the impression that there is cleavage or disharmony in the family. It is, therefore, imperative that every member of the family should play a responsible role to maintain the integrity of the unit. To be seen to operate in any way contrary to this norm arouses a general aversion and compels people to comment adversely and satirically on the issue.

Occasionally, the situation could lead to total rejection of a wife by her husband and the family. She may be taken back only with a strong assurance that she would change for the better. In the following example, a wife has been rejected by her husband because of her lack of team spirit and her relentless appetite for trouble. Her co-wives heap indignities on her and this humiliation is a deliberate attempt to embarrass her maximally.

Ihe anyị jiri jụ Mmaji
Bụ na Mmaji ji ngwere
Taa ya ji were noo
Ihe anyị jiri jụ Mmaji
Bụ n'Awusa bi n'Ihite n'ara Mmaji
Ihe anyị jiri jụ Mmaji omeke
Bụ na osikwasị ite
Ọ na enyo ọhụ ọkụ anyụọ
Ihe anyị jiri jụ Mmaji omeke
Bụ n'ikpu ya n'eru arịkwa

Why we rejected Mmaji
Is because Mmaji takes a lizard
Chews and swallows it like yam
Why we rejected Mmaji
Is because the Hausas at Ihite
Copulate with Mmaji
Why we rejected Mmaji, the recalcitrant one

Is because when she is cooking
She peeps into her vagina
While the fire dies off
Why we rejected Mmaji, the recalcitrant one
Is because her vagina grows worms.

The victim of the next satire is reputed to be quarrelsome and aggressive and her husband, finding it very difficult to bring her under control, has ordered that she leave permanently for her home. This extreme measure is necessary to ensure that social transgressions and vices are not encouraged. Her co-wives while deriding her and her family are also jeeringly summoning her parents to come and take her home.

Onye m gwara amarala
Onye m gwara amarala
Mgborie nwa Odimonu azụgbọkwa
Ị gbara ngwere nchanwụ
Odimonu bịa kpọrọ nwa gị
N'arụ o mere akarịala
Ụmụ Agbata ụmụ oji ọnụ
Nde n'eri awọ n'eri a n'ude
Ụmụ Agbata ụmụ oji ọnụ
Nde m gwara amarala.

She that I am referring to knows herself
She that I am referring to knows herself
Mgborie, daughter of Odimonu
Woe to you, you are a terrible person
Odimonu, come and take your daughter
Her abominations are innumerable
Children of Agbata, talkative people
Those that eat frogs in deep silence
Children of Agbata, talkative people
Those I am talking about know themselves.

MODERN WIVES

Another subject that constantly invites the satirical comment is the issue of 'modern' wives and their attitude generally. It is sometimes difficult for the older generation of women to comprehend the enormity of opportunities and modern facilities available to the younger ones. Part of the difficulty stems from the fact that just as the majority of the younger wives are educated, the majority of the older ones are not. This uneven status often results in a communication gap. The situation can assume extreme dimensions when mothers-in-law and daughters-in-law are directly concerned. However, the often less privileged older generation of women take it out on the younger ones by their constant satirical tauntings and scathing remarks.

As we shall see, the so-called "modern" wife is satirized for going to see the doctor for a pre-natal check - a facility that was hardly available to the older generation of mothers. Her offence is that the doctor has recommended that she step up on her protein consumption for her health and that of the baby.

Hei o ụmụ agbọghọ
Hei o ụmụ agbọghọ
Hei o agbọghọ ụdụhụ
Hei o agbọghọ ụdụhụ
Di m ejere m ụnọ ọgwụ
Di m ejere m ụnọ ọgwụ
Dọkịta ene m ahụ o
Sị m ribe akwa ọkụkọ
Na vọmvita n'anụ n'azụ o
Ka ya were nye m ọgwụ o
K' ọgwụ were gwọọ m ọrịa o
Hei ọna atụkwa ụnụ egwu o
Hei o ụmụ agbọghọ
Hei o agbọghọ ụdụhụ

Hei o young women
Hei o young women
Hei o young women of nowadays
Hei o young women of nowadays
My husband, I went to the hospital
My husband, I went to the hospital
The doctor examined me
And told me to be eating eggs
And bournvita and meat and fish
For him to give me some drugs
So that the drugs would cure my ailments
Hei does this not terrify you?
Hei o young women
Hei o young women of nowadays.

Some of these wives are employed as nurses, teachers, and workers in government parastatals, and because of the nature of their professions, they have little time to actively participate in farm work and at funerals. Some of the funerals are fixed on weekdays and they can only participate after work. Actually the main centre of criticism is the impact of modern trends which they are alleged to have almost totally embraced and which, the people are convinced, have been responsible for their lackadaisical attitude to some aspects of the traditional life. The following song was sung against working class women during a funeral. The purpose of the song is to bare the deviant attitudes of these wives and cause them to bow to the demands of the traditional society.

Nde okpu wigi eje ọrụ
Ụnụ ja ejekwa ọrụ eje
K'ọbụ eweta okụkoriọm
Ụnụ afụghaba ọnụ ihu
Ụmụ agbọghọ ọgba wọchị eje ọrụ
Ụnụ j'atakwa ego ata
K'ọbụ eweta okụkoriọm
Ụnụ afụghaba ọnụ ihu
Ụmụ agbọghọ oyi waịtị eje ọrụ
Kwanịa nị onye nwụrụ anwụ
K'ọbụ eweta okụkoriọm
Ụnụ eburu ya n'isi
Ụmụ agbọghọ oyi sketị eje akwa
Ụnụ akwagwene onye nwụrụ anwụ
K'ọbụ eweta okụkoriọm
Ụnụ eburu ya n'isi.

Those who wear wigs to the farm
Will you still go to the farm?
Or is it when there is a quarrel
You curl up your lips
Young women who wear watches to the farm
Will you chew money there?
Or is it when there is a quarrel
You curl up your lips
Young women who wear whites to the farm
Do join in mourning the dead
Or is it when there is a quarrel

You curl up your lips
Young women who wear skirt to a funeral
Have you mourned the dead?
Or is it when there is a quarrel
You become the ring leaders.

There is a general tendency for people to feel that 'modern' wives are not sufficiently committed to the activities going on in the village and would tell them so at the least provocation. Communal activities usually demand collective participation and any group that is identified as non-conforming becomes a satirical target. Since the village square serves as a recreative centre, the onus of cleaning it rests with the women. It is during some of such communal activities that they satirically taunt their working class counterparts who may ask to be excused because of their professional commitments. One of the most popular satirical songs directed at these women was recorded by the author who had the advantage of taking part in the activity as a participant observer.

Nde kwasịrị kwasịrị
Nọ n'enu mgbago
Ụnụ atụkwasịna ha obi
Ụmụ nwanyị nọ n'enu mgbago
Ụnụ atụkwasịna ha obi
Nde kwasịrị kwasịrị
Ha bụ akwa ọkụkọ
Ọ daa n'ana ọkụwasịa
Nde jara eji ume ọrụ
Atụkwasịna ha obi

Those unreliable people
Who live up the street
You should not count on them
The women who live up the street
You should not count on them
Those unreliable people
They are raw eggs
If they fall on the floor, they are smashed
Those who have no stamina for work
Do not count on them.

So far, this chapter has been preoccupied with the predominant themes of Ihiala satirical songs. We have observed how the people use and appreciate their satires and the impact of satire among the people. We have observed, also, a wide range of satire, from gentle and indirect criticism to severe attack bordering on invective. Our observation suggests that satirical participants and commentators do not attempt to achieve reform in the satirized. Rather, they are interested in self expression and in the amusement of the audience.

NOTES

1

D.I. Nwoga, "The Igbo Poet and Satire," in *Oral Poetry in Nigeria,* eds. U.N. Abalogu and others (Lagos: Nigeria Magazine, 1981), 233.

2

See note 1 above.

3

It is usual for the young bride to be presented with gifts on her first visit to her husband's home. These gifts would include articles of clothing, salt and soap. When she returns home, callers at her house are usually presented with token gifts of salt or a piece of soap.

4

A sneering kind of laughter.

5

R.N. Egudu, "Igbo Traditional Poetry and Family Relationships," *African Studies* Vol. 32, No. 1 (1973): 18.

6

G.T. Basden, *Niger Ibos* (London: Frank Cass and Co. Ltd., 1966), 228.

7

The statement connotes her readiness for sexual intercourse at all times.

8

Onomatopoeic word depicting the frivolity of the gossip.

9

Nasal sound signifying resentment.

10

It helps to achieve musical effect.

11

Onomatopoeic word signifying the restless movement on the bed caused by hunger and frustration.

12

A wooden platform constructed above the fireplace used mainly for storing food items.

CHAPTER SIX

THE TRANSFORMATION AND PERFORMANCE OF IHIALA SATIRE

The purpose of this chapter is to trace the development of satire in Ihiala from its beginnings as a weapon for the propagation of moral and social control to its present function as an aesthetic/entertainment tool. In tracing this development we shall analyse the early form of satire in Ihiala and the factors that helped to change the context in which satire was practised. The ultimate cause of this development was colonial contact - a factor that provided the impetus for the reappraisal of many aspects of the social system.

THE EARLY FORM OF SATIRE IN IHIALA

Satire was practised in its crudest form in Ihiala before the colonial era. It was a legitimate weapon for the punishment of people who had committed a variety of offences in the community. The intensity of punishment or societal reaction depended on the crime or offence.

Since a clearly defined code of morals existed, infringements of the laws may have led to severe penalties being inflicted. Satire was a common weapon with which to punish all categories of offenders. Ihiala communities had, for instance, no prisons. Consequently, most criminal offenders, particularly those who had committed any of the abominations, were meant to endure satirical torments and were often ostracised or sold into slavery.

Because the range of offences invariably influenced the severity of punishment, satire had to be categorized into male and female.

(1)   Male satire (oke ikpe) was used to denounce major offences or crimes such as stealing and all abomination. An abomination is "a breach that is considered so hideous that it requires the intervention of the maximal unit of authority within which the offender operates and usually calls for a cleansing ritual."[1]

Some offences stand before others in magnitude. Three of such offences are murder (especially the killing of a kinsman), stealing (especially the stealing of seed yams after they have been planted), and incest. These are atrocious offences which violate the laws of man and nature. These satirical performances were inevitably accompanied by direct physical abuse.

(2)   Female satire (nwunye ikpe) was used to deride minor offences such as promiscuity, quarrelsomeness, laziness, etc. Female satire was not accompanied by physical assault but publicly used the name and attributes of the culprit to achieve satirical effects. These two categories of satires existed simultaneously, each serving its purpose whenever the need arose.

The advent of the colonial powers and their subsequent intervention in most of the existing cultural practices of the people finally forced satire to make a transition to a more 'civilized' and 'acceptable' form of criticism, the archetypal. Archetype in criticism, M.H. Abrams states,

> Is applied to narrative designs, character types, or images which are said to be identifiable in a wide variety of works of literature, as well as in myths, dreams, and even ritualized modes of behaviour.[2]

Archetypal satire, therefore, employs type characterization. The songs have already been composed and are sung at appropriate times and places. Some of the songs have been composed at a time so remote in history that their origins cannot be traced. Oludare Olajubu makes a similar assertion in "Yoruba Oral Poetry: Composition and Performance" by stating that the poems might "have been composed thousands of years ago, or very recently; the author might be known or unknown."[3]

Archetypal satires reinforce the device of indirection - a device which has been utilized by satirists of all ages because of the dangers that satire entails. Such were these dangers that Juvenal had to declare that he would write only of the dead. The impact of colonial presence in Ihiala brought alive those dangers to the community's satirists, thereby helping in the transition of the existing form of satire. In archetypal satire, the audience may or may not know who is being satirized, and that factor helps them to focus their attention on the songs, that is, on the art of criticism rather than on the object of criticism.

As has already been implied, certain offences hack at the main tissue of human communities in such a way that they threaten the well being of all their members. These rank high among what may be considered criminal offences. In Ihiala, the breach of an abomination, for instance, attracts more severe societal disapproval than the breach of the other types of social norms.

Since abominations were considered the gravest of offences, the culprits were usually meant to absorb satirical abuses in addition to other forms of punishment that would be inflicted upon them. The theft of yam, for instance, particularly if it had not germinated from the soil, is an abomination against the earth goddess and calls forth a chain of punitive measures. This would be in addition to the raucous satires and the ritual cleansing of the perpetrator.

Upon uncovering an abomination, a gong was beaten to publicize the offence and elicit widespread condemnation from the community. Then the culprit was subjected to all sorts of indignity such as being spat at, enduring a few blows and lacerations, and being dragged round the village followed by a huge crowd and a piece of yam hung around his neck. The culprit had to absorb all kinds of mockery and direct physical abuse. The humiliation that accompanied this crude display was intended to serve as a deterrent to prospective deviants.

When the author interviewed Anazodo Oti[4] about the authenticity of this early form of satire, he confirmed it and, in fact, narrated details of several cases of such displays, the most pathetic being a case of incest. The two culprits, in addition to the shameful parade and the venomous songs, were stripped naked and marched to the village stream where they were made to bathe in the full view of the mocking crowd. This public act was meant to begin the ritual cleansing process.

All abominations call for ritual cleansing. In Ihiala, the items to be produced for such rituals usually include one sheep, nine cocks, nine chicks, nine kolanuts, nine alligator pepper, etc. These items must be produced by the culprit and must be ritually sacrificed to appease the offended spirit before the culprit may be allowed to resume normal relations with members of the community.

So serious is the abomination of incest that, in her book, Pat U. Okoye gave a full account of how a case of incest was handled. It was a man's funeral and the 'Umuada' (daughters of the lineage) observed that the dead man's tongue stuck out. According to them, that meant that the dead man's wife had been unfaithful and unless she confessed her 'sins' her husband's corpse would be abandoned in the house. Terribly frightened by this prospect, the widow confessed that she had had sexual relations with some male members of the family.

> The content of her crime was "Ọlalụ Ọgwa" meaning 'she committed incest' (having carnal knowledge of another member of the family) . . . . Such a crime as she had committed was enough to have been the cause or at least part of the cause of her husband's death.[5]

The humiliated wife was forced to name her partners. After the confusion that ensued in the aftermath of the widow's disclosure, the corpse was buried. Then the 'Umuada' prevailed on the widow and her 'illicit lovers' to perform purification ceremonies.

> These must be done to propitiate the gods. The deceased man can never rest until the rituals of "ịkpụ alụ," that is, 'purification of abomination' are performed. The consequences of neglect of this tradition are far-reaching, for instance, it could result in inexplicable sudden deaths among members of the kindred. The 'Umuada,' as custodians of social discipline, take it upon themselves to save the rest of the community from such disasters. They enforce the punitive measures, rather with an inordinate relish, to prevent others from committing similar transgressions.[6]

In an interview, Brendan Odimegwu[7] told the author that all abhorrent offences evoked satire of the crudest form, something like satire of the hard, bitter, Juvenalian school. Robert Elliott declared that "Juvenal's allegiance is to a more "primitive" satirical mode."[8]

The interviewee further narrated how he witnessed the ruthless handling of a man alleged to have committed homicide. The gruesome treatment was indescribable. Eventually, the culprit was dragged to the evil forest (Ajọ Ọfịa) and abandoned for wild animals to devour. His was an offence against the earth and her goddess must be propitiated.

In *Things Fall Apart*, Achebe pointed out in his description of the calamity that befell Okonkwo after he killed Ikemefuna, that the Earth had decreed that Okonkwo's action was an offence on the land and

> If the clan did not exact punishment for an offence against the great goddess, her wrath was loosed on all the land and not just on the offender.[9]

Although attention has been drawn to only three cases, these should merely be seen as examples of the most extreme offences as found in Ihiala. Such offences evoke male satire.

There are, of course, whole ranges of non-criminal/non-fatal offences against people. Some of those offences have already been discussed in the preceding chapter. They include premarital pregnancy, abortion, co-wife rivalry, mother-in-law/daughter-in-law rancour, lazy husbands and wives, quarrelsome people, and oppressive foster-mothers. These offences are considered minor and evoke female satires. This is in recognition of the fact that in human relationships some degree of impropriety and misunderstanding are bound to exist.

Indeed, the involvement of people in inter-personal relationships in restricted environments is a natural phenomenon which conduces to violent verbal and physical expressions as people break societal norms and/or get in the way of others. In such cases satire serves as a tool for ensuring social control. Every society upholds certain types of behaviour and condemns others in an effort to achieve integration and solidarity.

Interviewing Okeke Ndukwe[10] on an earlier form of satire for non- criminal offences, the author was informed that all satires were meant to punish and hurt their victims in some way and, therefore, perpetuate the deterrent effect. The only difference was that for non-criminal offences, satirical punishment was restricted to mere verbal ridicule.

The informant further explained that formerly, in Ihiala, young people strove to do the bidding of their parents and chastity was cherished. It was respectable for both the bride and groom to be ignorant about matters of sex until their first official night together. Young girls restrained from premarital sexual experience due to social punishments in the form of satirical songs meted out at marriage to brides who were not virgins. That was why some girls would choose to die than be so shamed by risking the local method of effecting an abortion with its attendant hazards.

So cherished is virgin marriage in many Igbo communities that a case in *Arrow of God* lends support to the discussion. Achebe portrayed Obika's deep anxiety over his new bride, Okuata, as they set out to perform the sacrifice of coverture. Obika knew that after the sacrifice he would take his wife to his hut and was anxious about whether he would "find her at home" or whether he would, on the other hand,

> Learn with angry humiliation that another had broken in and gone off with his prize? . . . Obika had already chosen an enormous goat as a present for his mother-in-law should his wife prove to be a virgin. He did not know exactly what he would do if he found that he could not take it to her after all.[11]

To her husband's relief and pride, Okuata was "found at home" and so he arranged "to take the goat and other presents to her mother in Umuezeani for giving him an unspoilt bride."[12] Compare the turn of events in the Obika-Okuata story to that of another bride, Ogbanje Omenyi,

> Whose husband was said to have sent to her parents for a matchet to cut the bush on either side of the highway which she carried between her thighs.[13]

The above accounts would help the reader to appreciate the value of virgin marriage in Ihiala and in most Igbo communities.

Minor offences such as domestic feuds make it imperative that satirical songs be made of the feuding partners to help effect a change in them.

From the foregoing, one is made to understand the nature of the satirical practice in Ihiala before the colonial contact.

COLONIAL CONTACT

Adiele Afigbo, commenting on the colonization of the African continent in general, reiterated that European colonialists sought to obliterate African culture and separate identity and made a determined effort to alter the course of African cultural development and turn it into new channels.[14] The colonial masters thought some of the existing cultural practices to be barbaric and prevailed on the colonized to revisit and modify some of them. Francis Cardinal Arinze, in support of this view, maintains that the correct attitude is to review the "Igbo culture in order to see what should be retained, what should be modified, purified or elevated, and what should be rejected."[15]

In Ihiala, as in most Igbo communities, the social system underwent transformations during the period of colonial contact. Until the advent of the British, slavery was rampant in Ihiala and among the Igbo. By the turn of the 19th century, the presence of the white man had begun to have a profound impact on many aspects of Ihiala cultural life. The white man devoted the best energies of his life to the abolition of slavery and some of the deadly practices perpetrated by the Igbo. G.T. Basden noted that slavery was widespread among the Igbo and that

> Only by the advance of Christianity and civilization and the power
> of good government is the practice being stamped out.[16]

As the administrative and judicial machinery was being set up by the colonial powers, they had to take into consideration the mechanisms of sanction which were already in existence in the communities. The European colonial powers could not contemplate the total adoption of the existing cultural systems. Their ideas about the cultural practices did not dispose them to the wholesale adoption of them.[17] What emerged eventually was a policy which accepted aspects of the traditional systems or modified versions of them while rejecting others, particularly the inhuman ones.

C. Onyeka Nwanunobi discloses in his book that the main direction in Nigeria in the relationship between the traditional systems and the British system was proclamation No. 5 in 1900. This served to determine what traditional law was acceptable, what procedure was admissible and what type of punishment might be applied.[18] With the intervention of the white man, society formulated sanction mechanisms whereby it allowed and, indeed, expected an injured person to take action on his own to seek redress when his rights had been infringed upon.

The awareness of such rights helped put in decline some of the unorthodox practices which offend civilized behaviour and encroach on fundamental human rights. One would expect that the people of Ihiala would readily have thrown the white men out of their community for meddling with their social affairs and creating a vacuum in the continuity of their social system. Instead, the people concentrated on the advantageous side of their relationship with the foreigners. In fact, the white men were seen to be more than the instrument of education and discipline for the young. They mediated in disputes and tended the sick when the native doctors had failed.

The awareness of human rights and the establishment of a formalized legal system gradually curtailed the impunity with which the people satirized the deviants of the community. Criminal offenders were duly tried and appropriately punished. This development affected the frequency with which satire was practised. People were mindful of the implications of their actions as the culprit had the option of seeking redress in whatever form he preferred.

All these developments significantly weakened the original potency of satire and gradually set in motion the machinery that transformed the satirical practice. So strong was the white man's intervention that cases abound where satirical tormentors had to abandon their targets and disappear at the glimpse of a white man. Okafor Igwegbe[19] confirmed this point in an interview with the author and attested to having been a witness at some of such incidents.

THE TRANSFORMATION OF SATIRE IN IHIALA

The extensive changes that took place in the satirical practice can be attributed to the colonial contact as has already been stated. Through the combined effects of education and Christianity on the social life, new social values evolved. That is to say that through the general adoptions of Western ways of life, the people expressed a new social attitude. From the early 1900's the social system was considerably weakened by this new social attitude, which stripped satire of much of its original potency. It was not until the first five decades of the 20th century that the people of Ihiala became overtly antagonistic towards the early form of satire. The sanction by the majority of the community made satire's early form redundant.

While the perpetrators of satire nursed the hope that they could keep it alive, public attitude towards the practice had changed immensely. Also, Christian teachings of the love of one's neighbour had begun to undermine the worst forms of social oppression. In *A History of the Igbo People*, Elizabeth Isichei extensively discussed this wave of Christian enlightenment which swept a large portion of Igboland.[20] The European colonialists condemned the early form of satire as barbaric and, with the new Christian attitude towards it, it did not have a chance of survival.

As the Christian population grew larger and the power of the colonial administration became more widely felt, satire's initial power slackened considerably. Only occasionally, in the hinterland regions, far from the focus of the colonial glare, was satire practised in anything close to its early form. Even that was not to last, for a new social attitude was sweeping the whole of Igboland whose effect on some traditional practices could not be halted.

In the process of time, the perpetrators of satire accepted the inevitability of that loss and slowly began to direct its course towards entertainment. Entertainment had always been a secondary feature in the structure of the satirical ritual display. But now there was a reversal in the structure; entertainment became the primary feature, while the emphasis on reform, once the ritual mainstay of the satirical practice, became a minor element.

At this point it had become clear that satire had shed its original form and much of the force in its function. A major change had taken place, and the change is a factor in the development which transformed satire into an aesthetic/dramatic experience. The best way to present the change is to show how the old form of satire was reconciled with the new social attitude, that is, to illustrate how the initial structure was transformed to meet new performance needs.

The transformation of satire brought about an important phenomenon. A situation evolved in which the spectator had an objective awareness of the performance nature of the event while simultaneously being a subjective participant in the action. The balance of objective observation and subjective involvement is a necessary condition for the aesthetic/dramatic experience to take place. In this condition the people abandoned their totally subjective attitude towards satire as a moral weapon, and began to look at it from an objective stance, that is, as a form of entertainment realized by skilled performers or actors during a performance. With this major development the spectators ceased being primarily participants in a ritual and became instead audience members at a dramatic presentation. Satire had become a dramatic event.

Although the people of Ihiala have accommodated the transformation, they still retain some vestiges of the old satirical context; they still retain some of their cultural beliefs in satire. This moderates their objectivity and helps to explain the complex attitude of the people towards satire.

By the late 1950's satire's role had become primarily entertainment, and that became the vehicle through which its social functions were carried out. Because of the risks that satire entailed, it became safer to satirize culprits collectively rather than individually as was realized in the performances. It was quite clear that with the people having been made aware of how to use the foreign court system, particularly for libel suits, satire's scope was necessarily curtailed, and so the control it provided was curtailed as well. Eventually, satire was restricted to a discreet and collective form of attack which made it difficult for libel suits to be convincingly executed. Satire, as a last resort, had to seek full realization and impact within the scope of performance.

THE PERFORMANCE OF IHIALA SATIRES

The objective here is to describe and analyse satirical performances with a view to showing their aesthetics and meaning. In Ihiala, occasions such as traditional festivals and moonlit-night plays typically invite satirical performances. In the performances, artistic talents are put into visible and audible form through songs and dramatic sketches, which are performed to entertain as well as to ridicule and expose deviant behaviour in the community.

In the earliest times, the most common application of satire in Ihiala was for social reform, and ridicule and assault were its primary weapons. But while providing character-moulding devices, ridicule also served as a rich source of amusement. Satire's gradual development from a moral tool to an entertainment tool occurred because it succumbed to the pressures mounted by European colonialists for a cultural change.

Although the earliest forms of Ihiala satire have been discussed in the preceding chapter, it can bear repetition here because it will illuminate the argument. One important point about the satirical performance of Ihiala is that it usually constitutes part of a larger performance. We shall, at this juncture, examine satire's progression from the earliest times to set the pace for an understanding of the analysis of the performance aesthetics of the archetypal form of satire.

MALE SATIRE (OKE IKPE)

The performance of male satires is usually extemporaneous. As soon as a criminal offence or an abomination is committed, an alarm is raised attracting people to the scene. Immediately, satirical songs are begun about the culprit, usually from a repertoire of such songs already in existence. This is accompanied by physical assault and other condescending treatment. Members of the crowd know the songs as they might have been sung before to depict similar situations. The name and attributes of the culprit are worked into the appropriate places in a standard song to create the desired impact. Identical themes are repeated with different turns of phrase and great effects are achieved in that way. Some talented people in the crowd would spontaneously compose songs which would add to the existing repertoire of such songs.

FEMALE SATIRE (NWUNYE IKPE)

The performance of female satires is not extemporaneous, but planned. For instance, if a young girl has been discovered to be pregnant before marriage, members of her age-grade will initiate a public denouncement of the culprit's behaviour. Satirical songs are collected by the age-grade, who sing them during moonlit-night plays and other social gatherings. As soon as these songs are presented, they become public property and are sung by everybody - peer groups, women and children. In fact, the songs become available for all and sundry.

Members of the culprit's age-grade may feel insulted by the behaviour of their member and may intensify her punishment by embellishing the songs with embarrassing details of her personal life gathered from those close to her. In fact, as these songs circulate more novelties are added to them.

ARCHETYPAL SATIRE

Archetypal satires are pre-planned but names are rarely mentioned. The intervention of the early European colonialists contributed to the practice of satire in this form. They viewed the old form as crude and barbaric and so the archetypal form became the acceptable form for the satirical practice. There exists a wide range of archetypal satires, these having been accumulated from the repertoire of both male and female satires.

Since this form of satire employs type characterization, no one is singled out for special mention and embarrassment. People who have committed a type of offence are collectively derided. As in other satirical forms, the songs become public property as soon as they are presented and are sung by peer groups, women and children, and privately in people's homes.

The satirical performance does not require elaborate rehearsals, but some form of rehearsal is needed to acquaint the performer with the basic movements for performance. Traditional musical instruments are used and are assigned to those who have attained proficiency in the handling of such instruments. The common instruments are maracas (ọyọ) and musical pot (udu). The people who handle them are experienced and talented people and need little time to rehearse what would be sung. After some songs have been compiled and the compilers have agreed on the dancing patterns, they now present them before a larger group at the rehearsal.

This rehearsal is done at the venue of the performance just before the actual performance. The reason for this is that the performers do not necessarily need to master the dance patterns to achieve total satirical effects. As long as they have a basic idea of the dance pattern, their individual innovations are meant to enrich the performance. What is considered more important is the message that the performance conveys to the audience.

A satirical performance during a traditional festival will be used to exemplify this discussion. The "Ịda ji" is a festival associated with the yam. Within this larger festival there is a ceremony which is an entirely female affair. The festival is planned to herald the planting season. Membership in the female group is limited to young unmarried girls. During the ceremony, there is a profuse rendering of satirical songs and their performances.

The executive members of this group will consult with the custodians of the village, who decide when the festival will take place. The venue for the festival is the village square.

While the main festival was going on, the female group would start their own activity. First of all, they would block a major entry to the village square and line fresh palm fronds across it. They would demand token gifts of cash from people before they were allowed to pass. It is at this point that they began their operations by unleashing their venomous songs on erring members of the community, especially members of their age group. Because of risks involved, the archetypal form of satire is more appropriate here.

Before the activity begins, the girls chat and laugh with one another while looking forward to some great entertainment. It is seen as an occasion for the release of tension and the experience of a mental state different from that of their daily routine. The executive members would ask the group to form a circle with the lead singers and those who play the instruments at the centre. The actual performance begins when one of the executive members gives a signal to the lead singers to start a tune. As the tune is started, it is followed by hand-clapping and drumming on the musical pot. One of the lead singers then raises her voice:

O ji ose aha ime
Nkata ose o jezukwara gi
A nasụ nekwe
Ị ma n'ọbụ agbọghọ n'ahụ

She that uses pepper to terminate pregnancy
Will a basket of pepper be sufficient for you?
All the drumming and chorusing
Is surely on the woman's body.

With the song the performers begin to dance according to the rehearsed patterns and with appropriate additions to accommodate individual talents. It is through these movements, which are familiar to the community, that it is possible for them to understand what is being enacted. Movements in satirical performance are not random. Every movement is objective, deliberate, interpretative and precise, and is designed to communicate.

At the mention of "A nasụ n'ekwe" the performers pretend to be beating the drum to depict the act of reckless sexual abandon which is being satirized. No effort is made to dance in a carefully rehearsed pattern. The point is that every performer is capable of dancing in a style that blends with the singing, the clapping and the drumming. As the dancing warms up, the singing and clapping and drumming attract other spectators to the scene. Their arrival causes the performers to perform more spiritedly.   The spectators would join the chorus and clap their hands.   Ropo Sekoni has observed that in any instance of such a performance, the singer and the audience

> Are not only concerned with the examination of the dominant values
> of their community but are also interested in the encapsulation of
> such discourse in an aesthetic form.[21]

Since the song will dictate the type of movement, the performers make body movements that demonstrate disapproval of the emotions implied in the song.   The spectators, having become participants in the performance, try to imitate the continuous body movements of the performers.   Because the performers and the spectators belong to the same community and may know the culprit, some spectators may engage in a discussion of him/her while the performance is going on. Enoch Mvula makes a similar point in his analysis of the "Performance of Gule Wamkulu" where he reiterates that:

> Members of the audience know each other and are aware of the
> events which have been the source of much gossip in the village. . . .
> Some of them talk to each other, indicating that the song refers to so
> and so who is among the crowd. They point at him and laugh as the
> performance goes on.[22]

As the performance gains momentum, the performers and the spectators intensify their clapping of hands and singing of the chorus in response to the rhythm of the song, the sound of the instruments, and the clapping of the hands.   They move their hands, legs, heads, shoulders and necks in unison with the song and hand-clapping as the performance builds to a climax.   The spirited dancing causes dust to rise (during the dry season) as the performers sweat and the spectators cheer and laugh heartily.

The chorus enables the spectators to participate in the performance.   Most often, there is repetition of some lines which contributes to the rhythm and substance of the song and the performance.   The lead singer may use facial or oral expressions to delineate the character of the satirical butt.   For instance, she may enlarge her eyes to depict excitement or twist her mouth to depict anger - all to the amusement of the spectators.

The ability to sing satirical songs does not detract from one's social status. If anything, it temporarily uplifts the singer's standing in the community - if only for as long as the performance lasts - because a talented singer/performer enjoys the undivided attention of his/her audience. Hence, during an outstanding performance he is held in high esteem by his audience. The author's investigation, however, did not provide any evidence to suggest that the ability to sing and perform satires well conferred high status on the singers outside a performance situation.

It should be recognized that what the singer is singing is given prominence over the accompaniment. The volume of the accompaniment is reduced when the words of the song have a specific message. The singer articulates his/her words for the audience. The song and the accompaniment alternate; when one is high the other is low. At the end of the song, the accompaniment gathers momentum and the performers dance until the lead singer either starts the song from the beginning or changes to another song.

Outside their performances certain artistic qualities of the songs are unfortunately lost. The written versions have been stripped of, among other things, the pace, cadences, rhythms, tone and mood of actual performances. The tone is an essential aspect of satirical songs. Lost also outside their performances are poetical qualities and the general atmosphere pervading the chanting of the songs. As a result, it is difficult to fairly assess the poetic qualities of the songs that are recorded for this book. It is perhaps impossible to accurately record all that is involved: the movements, the facial expressions, the dramatic actions and dance, the mimicry, etc.

The aesthetics of a satirical performance could be said to derive from the rhythmic clapping of the hands; the rhythmic body movements; the singing; the language of the songs; the facial expressions to depict a variety of moods; the participation of the spectators and their imitation of the performers - all of which blend to contribute to the beauty and the semantic content of the song and the performance.

NOTES

---

[1] C. Onyeka Nwanunobi, *African Social Institutions* (Nsukka: University of Nigeria Press, 1992), 154.

[2]

M.H. Abrams, *A Glossary of Literary Terms* (New York: Holt, Rinehart and Winston Inc., 1957), 11.

[3]

Oludare Olajubu, "Yoruba Oral Poetry: Composition and Performance," in *Oral Poetry in Nigeria,* eds. U.N. Abalogu and others (Lagos: Nigeria Magazine, 1981), 71.

[4]

Anazodo Oti, interview by author, tape recording, Ihiala, 15 January 1990.

[5]

Pat U. Okoye, *Widowhood: A Natural or Cultural Tragedy* (Enugu: Nucik Publishers, 1995), 86.

[6]

Okoye, 87.

[7]

Brendan Odimegwu, conversation with author, Ihiala, 3 April 1990.

[8]

Robert C. Elliott, *The Power of Satire: Magic, Ritual, Art* (New Jersey: Princeton University Press, 1960), 115.

[9]

Chinua Achebe, *Things Fall Apart* (London: Heinemann, 1958), 87.

[10]

Okeke Ndukwe, conversation with author, Ihiala, 31 May 1990.

[11]

Chinua Achebe, *Arrow of God* (London: Heinemann, 1964), 146.

[12]

Achebe, 151.

[13]

See note 12 above.

14

Adiele Afigbo, "Towards a cultural Revival Among the Igbo-Speaking Peoples" in *Igbo Language and Culture,* eds. Ogbalu and Emenanjo (Ibadan: University Press Ltd., 1982), 3.

15

Francis Arinze, "Christianity and Igbo Culture," in *Igbo Language and Culture,* eds. Ogbalu and Emenanjo (Ibadan: University Press Ltd., 1982), 193.

16

G.T. Basden, *Among the Ibos of Nigeria* (London: Frank Cass and Co. Ltd., 1966), 230-231.

17

C. Onyeka Nwanunobi, *African Social Institutions,* 157.

18

Nwanunobi, 159.

19

Okafor Igwegbe, conversation with author, Ihiala, 23 Ausgust 1991.

20

Elizabeth Isichei, *A History of the Igbo People* (London: The Macmillan Press Ltd., 1976), 115.

21

Ropo Sekoni, "The Narrator, Narrative-Pattern, and Audience Experience of Oral Narrative Performance," in *The Oral Peformance in Africa,* ed. Isidore Okpewho (Ibadan: Spectrum Books Limited, 1990), 142.

22

Enoch S.T. Mvula, "The Performance of Gule Wamkulu," in *The Oral Performance in Africa,* ed. Isidore Okpewho (Ibadan: Spectrum Books Limited, 1990), 91-92.

CHAPTER SEVEN

FORMAL TRAITS IN IHIALA SATIRE

African oral literature employs sophisticated literary and artistic devices. Since satire is an area of oral literature, Ihiala satire also utilizes these devices. We shall examine these devices with the objective of demonstrating that they have literary merit. Poetic devices abound in Ihiala satire. These devices bear testimony to the literariness of the satires. They also legitimise the relationship between poetry and satire in general. The predominance of some of the devices, however, varies according to cultural values and environment. The more obvious devices in Ihiala satire are: metaphor, simile, irony, onomatopoeia, hyperbole, repetition, traditional bluntness and proverbial usage. We shall now examine these poetic devices. There is, however, a preponderance of sexual imagery in the songs dealing with metaphor, simile, and traditional bluntness.

METAPHOR

Metaphor implies comparison between two unlike entities, as distinguished from simile, an explicit comparison signalled by the words 'like' or 'as.' Metaphor makes a leap from a reasonable comparison to an identification or fusion of two objects, to make one new entity partaking of the characteristics of both. Many words which were originally vivid images exist now as dead metaphors whose original aptness has been lost. Thus, metaphorical language develops continuously in complexity just as ordinary language does.

Metaphor may perform varied functions from the mere noting of a likeness to the evocation of several associations; it may exist as a minor element or may be the central concept and controlling image of the work. In *Tell Freedom,* for instance, Peter Abrahams generously uses the metaphorical device to add beauty and concreteness to his descriptions. The most memorable of these metaphors occurs in the last lines of the book:

> I walked briskly down to the docks.
> And all my dreams walked with me.[1]

Here, dream is not only personified into a walking being but it is also made to symbolize Peter Abrahams's ambition to escape into freedom in order to become a great writer who would "tell freedom."

Metaphor contributes to the portrayal of the beauty of Igbo satirical songs. The wealth of the Igbo language derives from the profuse use of metaphors in both oral speeches and oral poetry and satirical singers employ metaphors to embellish their expressions. Let us examine the following song:

> Ọkwa atụrụna fefuo
> Onye ma m'ọbụ obu j'abịa nị ọzọ
> Obu tụrụ pụọ ụchịcha abata
> Efere mkwuchi ekpugheena na njọ
> Ị jeenanị izu nị tọkịrị na mpio

> The patridge has tasted and has flown away
> Who knows whether the cuckoo will come next
> After the patridge, the cockroach will come
> The dish has been opened recklessly
> You went to steal but got trapped in the hole.

In this metaphor-laden satire, the words 'ọkwa' (patridge), 'obu' (cuckoo), and 'ụchịcha' (cockroach) all personify human beings who have defiled the satirical butt. The song suggests that the satirical culprit is public property and is available for the asking. Her reckless sexual activities are likened to the reckless 'opening of a dish.' As has been discussed in chapter five, the 'dish' should not be 'opened' before marriage. Here the dish creates an image of fragility and desecration. In the last line, premarital sex and the resultant pregnancy are likened to stealing and being caught. These point to the fact that apart from their literal meanings these words have deeper layers of meaning.

In another example, the satire is extended to close relatives of a compulsive thief. One of his relatives is described in the satire as:

Odiokpu, ụsụ tịntị n'ata ọji.
Odiokpu, small bat that chews the iroko tree.

In the line above, the metaphor has been used to characterize Odiokpu as a bat, that is, a mischievous character. Just as the bat is incapable of making a remarkable impact on the iroko tree by chewing it, so is Odiokpu incapable of exerting a positive influence on the behaviour of the culprit. The implication is that he is a beneficiary of the never-ending loot.

One more example of the use of metaphor occurs in the following lines.

A nasụ n'ekwe
Ị ma n'ọbụ agbọghọ n'ahụ.

The drumming and chorusing
Surely are on the woman's body.

The satire which indicts a young woman for profligacy has nothing to do with music. The drumming and chorusing have been introduced to create a mental picture of the sheer abandon with which she embraced the sexual act and to help the audience to mentally visualize the act. The importance of metaphor in Ihiala satirical art is that it helps the singer to achieve a diversity of expression. The aesthetic significance of the metaphors can be assessed by the lucidity, the picturesqueness, and the compression that the singer's expressions gain through these mental pictures.

SIMILE

A simile is a comparison between two distinctly different things and is indicated by the word 'like' or 'as.' The implication here is that a simile compares two completely different things focusing on the characteristics which they share. For instance, if we say that a man is "as meek as a lamb," we are trying to compare two completely different animals and also trying to identify the distinct quality which they have in common. In this case, meekness is the distinct quality which the man in question shares with the lamb.

Simile is an indispensable element in all literature. In the opening of *Things Fall Apart*, Achebe informs us that "Okonkwo was as slippery as a fish out of water . . . . In the end Okonkwo threw the Cat."[2] Here, Achebe uses simile to describe Okonkwo's wrestling prowess by comparing him to a fish.

Igbo traditional poets achieve a richness of style and create total effects through the use of similes. Let us now examine a few songs in our collection. In one of the songs on abortion, the singer sings:

Qcha nwa Mgbokwa
Qcha gha gha gha
Qbunwa qcha n'qbu ekpenta
Ikpu agbabagi aku mbe

The colour of Mgbokwa's daughter is terrible.
It is no more light skin
It is leprosy.
There is no hair on her vagina
It is like that of a tortoise.

In the above song, the singer compares the colour of the girl's skin to leprosy, a disease which in most Igbo communities is politely referred to as 'white skin.' This euphemism for leprosy is necessitated by a primitive belief that if the disease is called by its proper name it would automatically afflict the caller. The simile can be seen in the comparison of the girl's skin colour to leprosy. The change of colour of her skin occurred as a result of the pregnancy which she is desperate to terminate. Again, a simile occurs with the comparison of the bareness of the girl's pubic region to that of the tortoise. The bareness suggests that she is not richly endowed with feminine features expected of a mature woman.

We notice the use of simile in the following satire against a difficult and callous daughter-in-law:

Nwunye nwa m, omeke ejim
Ogwu azu gbadoro n'akpiri

My daughter-in-law, the callous one
Fish bone that gets stuck in the throat.

In the above song, the daughter-in-law's difficult traits are compared to fish bone. This is to say that just as fish bone causes pain and discomfort to the person in whose throat it is stuck, so does this daughter-in-law's unexemplary behaviour cause pain to those who encounter her on a daily basis.

Another instance of the use of simile is given in:

Echiena m eze
Eze nwogongolo

I have been crowned a king
King of praying mantis.

The simile occurs in the comparison of the chieftaincy to the praying mantis. The singer satirizes and ridicules the one who crowned himself a king. The image of a praying mantis is introduced to portray the fickle transiency of the chieftaincy struggle which has caused serious division and disaffection in the community and threatens its social foundation.

The comparisons have been successful in registering an impression of the satirical culprits on the audience's imagination. This imagistic device abounds in satirical poetry and indeed in all poetry. In Coleridge's "The Rime of the Ancient Mariner," the narrator states:

We stuck, nor breath nor motion;
As idle as a painted ship
Upon a painted ocean.[3]

In the above poem, the narrator compares his ship standing motionless on the sea to an artist's painting of a sailing ship.

One can, therefore, conclude that the validity of similes is justified by the method in which they help to project meaning beyond expression. They help the poet to communicate his thoughts to his audience in concise language rather than in long stretches of prose expressions. They also contribute to the memorability and suggestiveness of the satires.

HYPERBOLE

Rhetorical exaggeration is a unique feature of satirical poetry. Hyperbole or extravagant exaggeration simply means blowing up an object or idea more than its usual proportion. The technique has the power of making the satire very biting and sarcastic. Quite often, the victims of satire are infuriated, not just because their offences have been exposed, but because they have been outrageously exaggerated. The practice applies to practically everything that can be subjected to exaggeration, for instance, man, animals, ideas, incidents, etc. Instances of hyperbole abound in literature of all ages.

In *Arrow of God*, when Edogo brought a calabash of palm wine before his father, Ezeulu, and Akubue, his friend, Ezeulu asked:

> And why do you bring it in the presence of this my friend who
> took over the stomach of all his dead relatives?[4]

Ezeulu employed the device of hyperbole to portray his friend's incredible capacity for the consumption of palm wine.

Let us examine a few more instances in our collection. The technique of hyperbole is evident in the following satirical song collected at the funeral of a woman allegedly neglected and man-handled by her daughters-in-law:

> Onye akwanyere n'ọkụ
> K'ama ha ama ebe
> Onye e tiwuru n'aka
> K'ama ha ama ebe
> Onye azọwuru n'ụkwụ
> K'ama ha ama ebe.
>
> She that was pushed into a fire
> They are shedding crocodile tears for
> She that was beaten to death
> They are shedding crocodile tears for
> She that was trodden to death
> They are shedding crocodile tears for.

The woman in the above song is alleged to have died as a result of a fight with one of her daughter's-in-law. Whether there was an actual fight or not is another matter. The point is that at the moment of performance of the satire all the allegations commanded belief. The above situation is even more striking coming from a community in which mothers-in-law have been known to have the upper hand in their relationships with their daughters-in-law. One is expected to actually imagine the victim paying the supreme price at the hands of her daughter-in-law. That negates the concept of Igbo family life which thrives on absolute solidarity on the part of all its members. The element of hyperbole in the song is in the distortion of the extent of the rancour which existed among the parties concerned. Romanus Egudu, however, raises an important point by pointing out that within the family, relationships may be "amicable or antagonistic depending on the situation that motivates and orients attitudes to other people."[5] But Egudu goes on to say as he illustrates significant features of Igbo family life that:

> Atomistic existence is not as much as tolerated; for it is believed that "unity is strength." So that in one's relationships, this unity must be ensured against all destructive factors.[6]

Exaggeration, therefore, seems to be an effective weapon of securing the satirical culprits' attention and, perhaps, of reminding them of their expected roles as custodians of their community's morality.

The technique of hyperbole in satirical expressions could further be illustrated with the song below:

Onye ekwena nwa ya puta obodo
Okwundu g'eburu ya kpo ya okiri
Onye ekwena nwunye ya puta obodo
Okwundu g'eburu ya kpo ya okiri
Onye ekwena eghu ya puta obodo
Okwundu g'eburu ya kpo ya okiri

Let nobody allow his child to come out
Okwundu will mistake him for a he-goat
Let nobody allow his wife to come out
Okwundu will mistake her for a he-goat
Let nobody allow his goat to come out
Okwundu will mistake it for a he-goat.

The song is a satire against a man who has been caught in the act of stealing a goat. The act of stealing is in itself an offence but the singer grossly exaggerates this case. The warning that children, women and goats should be kept in-doors implies that the thief is capable of stealing anything or anybody. The singer provokes much laughter in the audience by making it imagine the thief pouncing on a human being in an attempt to steal him.

Another instance of hyperbole occurs in the song satirizing the incongruous fashion of the youth:

> Nwa agbọghọ yi itepu
> Sị n'ọbụ afe
> Ọ kọọ ọkọ n'isi
> Ịfụ akụ gbara ya n'ikpu.

> Young woman
> She wore a blouse
> And said it was a dress
> If she scratches her hair
> You will see her pubic hair.

Although the above song has been grossly exaggerated, the ever-changing fashion of youth has been a matter for concern to parents and adults. After the Nigerian civil war, which ended in 1970, the miniskirt was in vogue, and young girls who wore miniskirts automatically became satirical targets. The above song is a typical satire on a girl dressed in a miniskirt. The hyperbole is apparent in the reference to her dress which the singer calls a blouse because of its length; if she raises her hand, which would further pull up the short dress, her pubic region would be exposed. The singer seeks to elicit the appropriate response from the audience by making it visualize the short dress. The effect of this satirical piece clearly lies in the method of its presentation.

ONOMATOPOEIA

Onomatopoeia can be used in two senses, the narrow and the broad. In the narrow, and the more common sense, onomatopoeia is applied to a word, or group of words, whose sound seems to resemble the sound it denotes. In the broad sense, according to Abrams, onomatopoeia

Is applied to words or passages which seem to correspond to what they denote in any way whatever - in size, movement, or force, as well as sound.[7]

The Igbo language is replete with onomatopoeia because the language is tonal and tone plays an important role in determining the meaning of words. Igbo satirical singers make maximum use of this aspect of the language. An instance of the use of onomatopoeia can be seen in the song:

Ọ nakpọ rụrụrụ
Ọnata zụghụ zụghụ
Ọ nama ririri

There was commotion
She ate in profusion
She trembled all over.

The words 'rụrụrụ' (commotion), 'zụghụzụghụ' (profuse), and 'ririri' (trembling) are onomatopoeic and indicate and echo the intensity of the emotion which they represent.

Another instance of the use of onomatopoeia can be seen in the following song:

Ayarakiridim bụ agha
A nụhaa kiridim anyị abịa
Ayarakiridim bụ agha

Ayarakiridim is war
Once we hear kiridim
We come out
Ayarakiridim is war.

In the above song, the words 'ayarakiridim' and 'kiridim' are, again, onomatopoeic and are used to suggest and evoke the fury which is a usual characteristic of all wars.

The use of onomatopoeia can further be illustrated with the next song:

Ịgharajam ịgharajam n'ute
Ịgharajam ịgharajam n'ogoburu
Ịgharajam anụ aba ya n'aka

Igharajam azụ aba ya n'aka
Uwaegbunam n'agba ọkpụ rịghịrịghị

Igharajam igharajam on the mat
Igharajam igharajam on the bed
Igharajam no meat enters her hand
Igharajam no fish enters her hand
Uwaegbunam wriggles her waist.

The above song satirizes lazy wives who depend on their husbands to provide everything. It is a description of the frustrated movements of an over-dependent wife who must toss about in bed on an empty stomach until her husband returns to provide food. The word 'igharajam' is onomatopoeic signifying the sound of her movement on the bed. Also 'rịghịrịghị' is onomatopoeic indicating how she wriggles her waist from one side to the other.

One more instance of the use of onomatopoeia occurs in:

Nee ịhe tarawụza ya
N'eme ya n'ukwu
Ịwakam ịwakam.

See what his trousers
Are doing on his waist
Iwakam iwakam.

The onomatopoeic word 'ịwakam' leaves no doubt as to what the singer means as he throws his ankles out to represent the flopping around of the wide-bottom trousers.

From the foregoing, one could conclude that onomatopoeia is an important aesthetic quality of satirical poetry. It enhances and produces musical effect in Ihiala satire and in oral poetry in general.

REPETITION

Repetition is an important device in satirical songs. In most of the songs collected, repetition occurs either of a group of words or whole sentences. It is obvious that repetition is necessarily employed to gain emphasis. There are various forms of repetition in the songs but two kinds predominate. There are those repetitions that occur after one line and those that occur after two or more lines. Here is one that occurs after one line:

Onye ekwena nne ya pụta obodo
Okwundu ga eburu ya kpọ ya okiri
Onye ekwena ehi ya pụta obodo
Okwundu ga eburu ya kpọ ya okiri
Onye ekwena ezi ya pụta obodo
Okwundu ga eburu ya kpọ ya okiri.

Let nobody allow his mother to come out
Okwundu will mistake her for a he-goat
Let nobody allow his cattle to come out
Okwundu will mistake it for a he-goat
Let nobody allow his pig to come out
Okwundu will mistake it for a he-goat.

This type of repetition is quite common in Ihiala satirical songs.

The second type of repetition, those that occur after two or more lines, can be illustrated with the following song:

Enyi m nwanyị
Nwa onye ọdịịrị mma
Ama m onye ịbụ
Ị na asụ m asụ
A na m eghe gi eghe
Ama m onye ịbụ
I kwuru m pụba ezi
E kwuru m gị baba ụnọ
Ama m onye ịbụ

My woman friend
Child of the contented one
I know you for what you are
If you are pounding me
I am frying you
I know you for what you are
If you discuss me outside
I discuss you inside
I know you for what you are.

Another example of the above type of repetition is given below:

Ihe anyị jiri jụ Mmaji

Bụ na Mmaji ji ngwere
Taa ya ji were noo
Ihe anyị jiri jụ Mmaji
Bụ n'Awụsa bi n'Ihite
N'ara Mmaji
Ihe anyị jiri jụ Mmaji
Bụ na osikwasị ite
Ọna enyo ọhụ

Why we have rejected Mmaji
Is because she takes a lizard
Chews and swallows it like yam
Why we have rejected Mmaji
Is because the Hausas at Ihite
Copulate with Mmaji
Why we have rejected Mmaji
Is because when she is cooking
She peeps into her vagina.

The above songs illustrate the effect of repetition on the audience. Repetition encourages the audience to participate in the performance by repeating the refrain together with the singer. Repetition also enhances the poetic quality of the satires by making them both rhythmic and sonorous, which also emphasizes the subject of discussion.

IRONY

Irony is a language device either in spoken or written form (verbal irony), in which the real meaning is concealed or contradicted by the literal meanings of the words, or in a theatrical situation (dramatic irony) in which there is an incongruity between what is expected and what occurs. Verbal irony arises from a sophisticated or resigned awareness of contrast between what is and what ought to be and expresses a controlled pathos without sentimentality. It is a form of indirection that avoids overt praise or censure.

Irony is a common device in satirical poetry. An instance of irony can be seen in the example below:

Ama nnekwu mere ịhea
Ọbụ ọbụrụ ọkeọkpa
Anyị ajara ama

Who knows which hen did this
If it were a cock
We would have known.

These ironical statements made during an inter-village conflict
are meant to inform the opponents that they are considered weak and
no match for any competition. They have been likened to a hen by
their opponents. The reference to a cock implies the superior status
which the enemy village has accorded themselves. In their pomposity
they have placed their rivals beside the weaker specie of a lower
animal, the hen. By this they seem to claim total superiority over their
rivals.

Another example of the use of irony is given in the song:

Nwunye di anyị gbakwa ọtọ ana
Jeenị nga odie were anya nene

Our co-wife is departing naked
Go where she is lying and see for yourself.

The irony is taken from a satire against an oppressive and
negligent husband. The first line suggests that the deceased was
actually naked. She was not. The irony was used to show how
oppressed and neglected the deceased had been and which may have
contributed to her death.

One more instance occurs in

Oji azụ arị akwa
Onye arụ k'ịbụ

She who climbs the bed with her back
You are an abominable person.

The irony comes from a satire by a jealous co-wife against a
younger rival. The first line implies her readiness for sexual
intercourse at all times. The jealousy of the aggrieved wife has been
sorely provoked because their common husband gives undivided
attention to his youngest wife. His exhibition of partiality is the root
cause of the rivalry between the two wives.

PROVERBS

Proverbs are succinct and pithy sayings in general use, expressing commonly held ideas and beliefs. They are part of every spoken language and are related to such other forms of folk literature as riddles and fables that have originated in oral tradition. Comparisons of proverbs found in various parts of the world show that the same kernel of wisdom may be gleaned under different cultural conditions and languages. Their first appearance in literary form is often an adaptation of an oral saying.

Ihiala satires are occasionally laced with subtle proverbs. Igbo oral poets make extensive use of proverbs. Proverbs usually have a didactic quality and can be used in literature to project a writer's theme. When appropriately used, proverbs achieve total effects and a richness of expression. Achebe, who has used this device profusely in his writings, affirms that:

> Among the Ibo the art of conversation is regarded very highly, and proverbs are the palm-oil with which words are eaten.[8]

Commenting on Achebe's use of proverbs, Bernth Lindfors states:

> Achebe's proverbs can serve as keys to an understanding of his novels because he uses them not merely to add touches of local color but to sound and reiterate themes, to sharpen characterization, to clarify conflict, and to focus on the values of the society he is portraying.[9]

Here is an example of a satirical proverb:

> Kama ǫgǫ m j'egbu m
> O gbuo onye m meere.

> Rather than be killed by my good act
> Let it kill my benefactor.

This proverb is satirizing a callous husband at the funeral of his wife. The deceased woman's relations have accused the husband of having caused the untimely death of his wife by his maltreatment of her. Through the medium of the proverb, the group hurls invectives at their brother-in-law, a means of voicing their dissatisfaction with the way he conducted the affairs of the marriage. The next song features another satirical proverb:

Oji ji agba ụtụtụ
Ji j'agwụ ụtụtụ akwakporo

She that eats yam for breakfast
Yams will soon finish
But mornings will stretch to infinity.

Because polygamy is deeply rooted in Igbo culture, the song from which this proverb is taken is a satire by a jealous co-wife against her husband and her latest rival. The young wife, who is enjoying the attention of a husband in a polygamous home, is being reminded by a co-wife that the attention she is getting is very transient. The aggrieved wife ought to know because she herself was once a latest arrival.

Another instance of the use of a proverb can further be illustrated with the following:

Onye bara nwa ya 'Nkemdịrịm'
Ọ sị nke onye fuo?

He who names his child 'May mine endure'
Whose own does he want to perish?

The above proverb is a satire against those who let their domestic animals loose to feed on other people's crops and property. In Ihiala, there is a law that if such animals are caught they should be taken to the village councillor where the owners must pay a certain sum of money before they can take them back. Yet, instances of domestic animals causing havoc in people's farms and homesteads abound. Such occasions seem appropriate for the aggrieved person to use the above proverb.

Here is one more instance of a satirical proverb:

Ogeri debere di
Orie na ndo ọnwa

She who waits for her husband
Eats at midnight.

The proverb satirizes lazy wives who are totally dependent on their husbands. A wife who folds her hands and waits for her husband to provide everything will find, to her dismay, that she is in perpetual misery. As the above proverb suggests, she is never sure of her food. She can only wait until her husband brings home something, probably at midnight, if at all. On the other hand, a less dependent or an industrious woman can afford certain basic conveniences for herself and her children. Husbands are expected to provide certain basic needs of the family, but it is not always so. The proverb is a wake-up call to wives to strive to be industrious.

TRADITIONAL BLUNTNESS

Traditional bluntness is characterized by a pre-occupation with obscenity. Traditional satirists are conscious of the need for verbal dexterity. This is why they are alive to the application of various language techniques that not only enrich their expressions but also capture the attention of their audience. Traditional bluntness contributes to the aesthetic significance of Igbo satirical art. It seems obvious from the songs that nothing is considered too indecent in traditional Igbo satirical art. Such things as the human genitalia are called by their proper names without being couched in euphemistic terms as in normal, everyday usage.

This unabashed use of such terms gives satire its immediate appeal and suggests disorder or chaos which appears to threaten existing social structures. Audiences are mildly and pleasantly shocked by the use of such terms and enjoy them for the sake of freedom and spiritual renewal by exceeding the boundaries of generally acceptable social behaviour. The main advantage is that it is sharp, direct, and makes direct reference to the object of satire. Since satire is virtually a spoken art, the use of traditional bluntness helps the audience to capture the essence of the satire without having to wade through symbolism, euphemism, etc. Below is an example:

Ihe anyị jiri jụ Mmaji
Bụ n'Awụsa bi n'Ihite n'ara Mmaji
Ihe anyị jiri jụ Mmaji
Bụ na osikwasị ite
Ọna enyo ọhụ ọkụ anyụọ

Ihe anyị jiri jụ Mmaji
Bụ na ikpu ya na eru arịkwa

Why we have rejected Mmaji
Is because the Hausas at Ihite
Copulate with Mmaji
Why we have rejected Mmaji
Is because when she is cooking
She peeps into her vagina
While the fire dies off
Why we have rejected Mmaji
Is because her vagina grows worms.

Here, traditional bluntness is suggested by 'ọhụ' and 'ikpu' both Igbo words for vagina. In other contexts an attempt could have been made to substitute them with less obvious terms. Mmaji's rejection stems from her promiscuous behaviour. Although married, she copulates with the 'Hausas' and her promiscuity leads her to 'peep into her vagina,' something that respectable people do not do, at least in public. The phrase implies a deeper layer of meaning which is not necessarily physical but connotes self examination. The culprit is being reminded to look inwards and assess herself. The fact that 'her vagina grows worms' implies that she is free for all and probably does not maintain a reasonable degree of personal hygiene. The use of traditional bluntness in the above song leaves little to the imagination.

The use of traditional bluntness is evident in the next song on premarital pregnancy:

Ọbụ ara nị dara ada k'ana ekwu
Ọbụ atụrụ jaana ekwe abịa n'ara
Ara dara ada n'omebigwo
Ara dara ada n'ozugo
Ọkwa nụ ogbe ikpu k'obu aga.

Is it the sagged breasts they are talking about?
If the vagina is not willing
Who will fuck it?
The sagged breasts are no more good
The sagged breasts are enough
Is it the broad vagina that she is parading?

Here, the satirical target is portrayed as a woman of easy virtue.

The second line of the song suggests her frequent willingness for sexual intercourse. The use of traditional bluntness apparent in the 'sagged breasts,' the 'broad vagina' and 'fuck' has aided the satirical singer to maximally degrade the target and slash her self esteem. She would lose the respect of her community and would have little to be proud of.

The seriousness of the above satire can never be fully appreciated unless one is made to understand that it comes from a community in which virgin marriage is cherished. Most Igbo communities expect young girls to uphold this moral virtue. Ambrose Monye sums up the importance of virgin marriage in Aniocha Igbo community in the following lines:

> Any young girl who got impregnated would go through the shame and pain of carrying the pregnancy till full term. So it took great moral restraint for a young lady to keep her virginity intact till she got married. . . . This explains the kind of joy and sense of pride which a young girl who remains a virgin till her marriage day enjoys.[10]

In yet another song, traditional bluntness is apparent:

Egoigwe jebere machari
Onyeka ejebe ikpughe ikpu

Egoigwe went to the mortuary
Onyeka went to open the vagina.

In this song, the singer uses the device to arouse curiosity and to whip up emotions. The mention of opening 'the vagina' was done to arouse due sentiments. The culprit exhibited extreme callousness and lack of respect for his deceased and senior wife. Her corpse is in the mortuary awaiting burial and instead of mourning, he accompanies his latest wife to a social ceremony. This gesture earned him the wrath of decent members of the community. The mention of 'mortuary' shows that the satire is a contemporary one. Until very recent times, the community buried their dead almost immediately.

The performers of these satires do not set out to arouse revulsion in the audience by their use of traditional bluntness. Rather, their aim is to humourize, enthral, and mildly shock the people and induce them to participate in the condemnation of the act in question.

This chapter has so far demonstrated that Ihiala satires, like those of the other cultures of the world, have literary qualities. Through examples of satires in our collection, some of the characteristics which the satires share with other literary genres were discussed and analysed. These characteristics help to buttress the argument that the satires have literary merit and deserve the attention of the literary scholar.

NOTES

1

Peter Abrahams, *Tell Freedom* ed. W.G. Bebbington (London: George Allen & Unwin Ltd., 1963), 224.

2

Chinua Achebe, *Things Fall Apart* (London: Heinemann, 1958), 3.

3

Samuel Taylor Coleridge, "The Rime of the Ancient Mariner," in *The Poet's World*, ed. James Reeves (London: Heinemann, 1972), 183.

4

Chinua Achebe, *Arrow of God*, (London: Heinemann, 1964), 119.

5

R.N. Egudu, "Igbo Traditional Poetry and Family Relationships," *African Studies* Vol. 32, No.1 (1973): 18.

6

Egudu, 21.

7

M.H. Abrams, *A Glossary of Literary Terms,* (New York: Holt, Rinehart and Winston Inc., 1957), 118.

8

Achebe, *Things Fall Apart*, 5.

9

Bernth Lindfors, "The Palm Oil With Which Achebe's Words are Eaten," *African Literature Today* 1 (1968): 6.

10

Ambrose A. Monye, "Women in Nigerian Folklore: Panegyric and Satirical Poems on Women in Aniocha Igbo Oral Poetry," in *Power and Powerlessness of Women in West African Orality*, Raoul Granqvist and Nnadozie Inyama, eds. (Sweden: The Printing office of Umea University, 1992), 64-65.

CONCLUSION

The author has examined the development of Igbo satire from its ritual origins to its present status as a form of social entertainment. In the earliest times, satire in Ihiala was principally used to propagate social reform, and ridicule and assault were its primary weapons. Consequently, the satirical singer was greatly feared. This reaction is not exclusive to the Igbo; it includes other African societies. In the process of time, there occurred a gradual loss of satire's initial power. This loss of power occurred partly as a result of European colonization - a factor that provided the standpoint for the reappraisal of several aspects of the culture. This reappraisal of the social system marked the beginning of the transition that satire ultimately had to make in order to continue to be practised in a society that had succumbed to colonial pressure.

The work has demonstrated how Ihiala satirical performances have been stripped of their ritual qualities. Although the forces of transformation could have affected the early form of satire, the colonial administration and missionary encounter helped in mounting pressure on the existing satirical tradition and so forced satire to change sooner to its present form.

While the European colonialists and missionaries were, consciously or unconsciously, stripping satirical performances of their ritual qualities, they were actually helping in the evolution of satire to its present status as an aesthetic and entertainment tool. Actually, aspects of entertainment had long been incorporated into the satirical ritual display, but it was not until the ritual content of satire was dropped that the actual transformation took place. The need to preserve the culture has necessitated the continued practice of satire in its present form, and when the form gained currency, the transformation became complete. This modified satirical form transformed the satirical performances from ritual activities to social entertainment and elevated the use of satire as a medium of social control in Ihiala.

This work reveals that it is during satirical performances that their aesthetic qualities can be fully appreciated. The performances are mainly held in the traditional communities and the participants continually introduce novelties that enhance the aesthetics of the performances.

Currently, a vast number of young people are migrating from the rural communities to urban centres. There is the fear that, in time, the villages will lose the manpower to organize satirical performances, thereby causing them to die a natural death. Pre-colonial Igbo society was not as disrupted and diffuse as it is today; there was no urbanization, no population drift, and cultural values were more or less static. In post-colonial Igbo society tastes have changed and cultural values have undergone enormous modifications.

Satirical performances are orally transmitted and have been so preserved. Only a negligible few have been committed to writing. It is important to find lasting means of preserving this aspect of traditional literature should there be a break in tradition so as to save the performances from total extinction. This idea has been summed up by Helen Peters in the following words:

> It would appear that . . . "our gold crop is sinking ungathered." It is still practised in the villages nonetheless but it is these same villages who have been drained of their population by the cities. . . .
> One would say, collect them and put them down in writing, that would preserve them forever. . . . Recording on tapes and discs are at present ways of collecting and preserving folk literature. . . . It can be proffered that filming as a collection device will capture the totality of the experience, words, audience, movement, facial expressions, etc.[1]

She stresses the inadequacy of writing alone as a way of preserving folk literature and maintains that it has to be subjected to such a preservatory form that would portray its life and art most accurately.

This work shows that although the concept of a corrective social function for satire is apparent in the songs, amusement is equally appreciated and, indeed, may be the fundamental impulse of satirical expression. Satirists are aware that some satirical culprits are incapable of change. Although satirical songs are inevitably made of them whenever they violate a social norm, whether the songs would actually effect the desired change in them is another matter. The satirical singer, however, feels content to jeer at and ridicule disapproveable social behaviour if only to deter potential deviants from treading the same path. In the absence of effecting a change in the culprit, the satirical singer is satisfied that he has been brought to "bitter contempt"[2] through the venomous songs.

Satire is a hazardous occupation. After the transformation of satire in Ihiala, the prevailing satirical form employed the device of indirection as its chief machinery of operation. It was no longer safe to practice satire in the old form since the targets could seek redress either by direct law suits or by physically attacking their tormentors. That is why the satirist's attack is in some way indirect, distorted and artful, suggesting caution or real unconcern with social reform. The device of indirection helps to direct the audience's attention away from the satirical target, that is, the object of criticism, to the art of criticism. For instance, during a satirical performance the performer's interest seems to focus on the audience's admiration of his/her actions, the body movements, the facial expressions, etc. In the act of modern Ihiala, and so Igbo, satirical performance, the singer is more concerned with the entertainment of the audience than with the correction of the satirical culprit. The singer seemingly directs his words at his target while his eyes are focused on the audience from whom he expects to be admired and approved.

This work has shown that the emphasis of the satirical activity has shifted from the correction of vice to emphasis on performance, on licensed entertainment for all and sundry. Although satire is being performed more frequently for entertainment than for reform, yet a sense of social function is still perceivable. Particularly in its traditional contexts, the notion of social control is apparent and is an essential component of the Igbo view of satire regardless of whether this notion is the motivation for practising it in all its various forms.

NOTES

[1]

Helen Peters, "Reflections on the Preservation of Igbo Folk Literature," *The Conch*, Vol. III, No.2, (1971): 101-102.

[2]

Gilbert Highet, *The Anatomy of Satire*, (Princeton: Princeton University Press, 1962), 156.

BIBLIOGRAPHY

Abraham, W.E. *The Mind of Africa*. Chicago: University of Chicago Press, 1962.

Abrahams, Peter. *Tell Freedom*. London: George Allen & Unwin Ltd., 1963.

Abrahams, Roger D. "Introductory Remarks to a Rhetorical Theory of Folklore." *Journal of American Folklore* 81 (1968), 143-158.

Abrams, M.H. *A Glossary of Literary Terms*. New York: Holt, Rinehart and Winston Inc., 1957.

Achebe, Chinua. *Things Fall Apart*. London: Heinemann, 1958.

_____. *No Longer at Ease*. London: Heinemann, 1960.

_____. *Arrow of God*. London: Heinemann, 1964.

_____. "Where Angels Fear to Tread," *African Writers on African Writing*, ed. G.D. Killam. London: Heinemann, 1973.

_____. *Morning Yet on Creation Day*. London: Heinemann, 1975.

Adedeji, Joel A. "Form and Function of Satire in Yoruba Drama," *Odu* 4, i (1967), 61-72.

_____. "Traditional Yoruba Theatre," *African Arts* 3, i (1969), 60-63.

_____. "Oral Tradition and the Contemporary Theatre in Nigeria," *Research in African Literatures* 2, ii (1971), 134-149.

Afigbo, A.E. "Towards a History of The Igbo-Speaking Peoples of Nigeria." In *Igbo Language and Culture*, eds. Ogbalu and Emenanjo. Ibadan: Oxford University Press, 1975.

_____. *The Warrant Chiefs*. London: Longman, 1972.

_____. *Ropes of Sand: Studies in Igbo History and Culture*. Ibadan: University Press Ltd., 1981.

_____. "Towards a Cultural Revival among Igbo-Speaking Peoples," *Igbo Language and Culture* 2 (1982), 1-14.

Akpabot, Samuel. "Musicology Approach to Efik/Ibibio Oral Poetry."

In *Oral Poetry in Nigeria*, eds. Abalogu, Ashiwaju and
    Amadi-Tshiwala. Lagos: Nigeria Magazine, 1981, 86-95.
Alagoa, E.J. "The use of Oral Literary Data for History: Examples
    from Niger Delta Proverbs," *Journal of American Folklore* 81
    (1968), 225-243.
Amankulor, J.N. "Traditional Black African Theatre: Problems of
    Critical Evaluation," *Ufahamu* 6, ii (1976), 27-46.
_____. "The Concept and Practice of the Traditional African Festival
    Theatre." Ph.D. diss., University of California, Los Angeles,
    1977.
_____. "Dance as an Element of Artistic Synthesis in Traditional
    Igbo Festival Theatre," *Okike* 17 (1980) 84-95.
Arinze, Francis. *Sacrifice in Igbo Religion*. Ibadan: Ibadan University
    Press, 1970.
_____. "Christianity and Igbo Culture," *Igbo Language and Culture* 2
    (1982), 181-197.
Arnott, K. *African Myths and Legends*. Oxford: Oxford University
    Press, 1972.
Austerlitz, R. *The Identification of Folkloristic Genres*. Warsaw:
    Pantwowe Hydawnic Two, 1961.
Awoonor, Kofi, trans., ed. "Poems and Abuse Poems of the Ewe,"
    Alcheringa 3 (1971), 1-15.
Azuonye, Chukwuma. "Stability and Change in the Performance of
    Ohafia Igbo Singers of Tales," *Research in African Literatures*
    14, iii (1983), 332-380.
Babalola, S.A. *The Content and Form of Yoruba Ijala*. Oxford:
    Clarendon Press, 1966.
Bascom, William R. "Verbal Art," *Journal of American Folklore*, 68
    (1955), 245-252.
_____. *The Yoruba of Southwestern Nigeria*. New York: Holt,
    Rinehart and Winston, 1969.
_____. and Melville J. Herskovits, eds. *Continuity and Change in
    African Cultures*. Chicago: University of Chicago Press,
    1959.
Basden, G.T. *Among the Ibos of Nigeria*. London: Frank Cass, 1966.
Bateson, F.W. *The Scholar and Critic*. London: Routledge and Kegan
    Paul, 1972.
Beattie, John. *Other Cultures*. New York: Free Press, 1964.
Beidelman, T.O. "Further Adventures of Hyena and the Rabbit: The
    Folktale as a Sociological Model," *Africa* 33 (1963).

Beier, Ulli, ed. *Yoruba Poetry: An Anthology of Traditional Poems.*
    Cambridge: University Press, 1970.
_____ ed. *Introduction to African Literature: an Anthology of*
    Critical Writings. London: Longman Group Ltd., 1980.
Ben-Amos, Dan, ed. *Folklore Genres.* Austin: University of Texas
    Press, 1969.
_____. and K.S. Goldstein, eds. *Folklore: Performance and*
    Communication. The Hague: Mouton and Co. Publishers,
    1975.
_____. "Analytic Categories and Ethnic Genres." In *Folklore*
    Genres, ed. Dan Ben-Amos. Austin: University of Texas
    Press, 1976, 215-225.
Berry, J. *Spoken Art in West Africa.* London: n.p., 1961.
Bloom, Edward A. and Lillian D. "The Satiric Mode of Feeling: A
    Theory of Intention," *Criticism* 9, ii (1969) 115-139.
Boorke, J.C. *Scatologic Rites of all Nations.* Washington: W.H.
    Lowdermilk, 1891.
Boswell, G.W. *Fundamental of Folk Literature.* Oesterhout:
    Anthropological Publications, 1962.
Botkin, B.A. ed. *A Treasury of American Folklore.* New York:
    Crown Publishers, 1944.
Bowra, C.M. *Heroic Poetry.* London: Macmillan and Co., 1952.
Bronislaw, Malinowski. *Magic, Science and Religion.* New York:
    Doubleday, 1954.
Brunvand, J.H. *Folklore: A Study and Researcher Guide.* New York:
    Martin's Press, 1976.
_____. *A Study of American Folklore: An Introduction.* New York:
    Mouton, 1968.
Burke, Kenneth. "Literature as Equipment For Living." In *The*
    Philosophy of the Literary Form ed. Kenneth Burke. New
    York: Vintage Books, 1957, 254-262.
Burn, Tom. "Folklore in the Mass Media: Television," *Folklore Forum*
    2, iv (1969), 90-106.
Byrne, D. *An Introduction to Personality Research, Theory and*
    Application. New Jersey: Prentice Hall Inc., 1974.
Chadwick, H. Munro and N. Kershaw Chadwick. *The Growth of*
    Literature, 3 vols. New York: Macmillan, 1940.
Chukwuma, Helen. "The Oral Nature of Traditional Poetry and
    Language," *Journal of the Nigerian English Studies*
    Association 8, i (1976), 12-22.
Clark, J.P. "Aspects of Nigerian Drama," *Nigeria Magazine* 89 (1966),

118-126.

Coffin, T., ed. *American Folklore*. New York: Frederick Praeger, 1968.

Coobes, H. *Literature and Criticism*. New York: Penguin Books, 1980.

Cook, Albert. *The Dark Voyage and the Golden Mean: A Philosophy of Comedy*. Cambridge Mass: Harvard University Press, 1949.

Courlander, Harold. *A Treasury of American Folklore*. New York: Crown Publishers, 1975.

Cox, G.W. *An Introduction to the Science of Comparative Mythology and Folklore*. London: n.p., 1881.

Crowder, Michael. "Tradition and Change in Nigerian Literature," *Tri-Quarterly* 5, (1966), 117-124.

Crowly, D.J. "The Uses of African Verbal Art," *Journal of Folklore Institute*, (1969),118-132.

Dadie, B.B. *Folklore and Literature*. London: n.p., 1964.

Dance, F.E., ed. *Human Communication Theory: Critical Essays*. New York: n.p., 1967.

Dathorne, O.R. *The Black Mind: A History of African Literature*. Minnesota: University of Minnesota Press, 1974.

Davidson, L.J. *A Guide to American Folklore*. Denver: University of Denver Press, 1951.

Dawson, J.L.M. and W.J. Lonner. *Readings in Cross-Cultural Psychology*. Hong Kong: Hong Kong University Press, 1974.

Doob, Leonard W., ed. *Ants Will Not Eat Your Fingers: A Selection of Traditional African Poems*. New York: Walker and Company, 1966.

_____. *Communication in Africa*. New Haven: Yale University Press, 1961.

Dorson, R.M., ed. *Folklore and Folklife: An Introduction*. Chicago: The University of Chicago Press, 1972.

_____. *American Folklore and the Historian*. Hatboro: Folklore Associates, 1964.

_____. *American Folklore*. Chicago: University of Chicago Press, 1959.

_____. *Folklore: Selected Essays*. Bloomington: Indiana University Press, 1972.

_____. *African Folklore*. Bloomington: Indiana University Press, 1972.

_____. "Current Folklore Theories," *Current Anthropology* 4 (1963),

93-112.

Drew, Elizabeth. *Discovering Drama*. New York: W.W. Norton Publishers, 1937.

Duerden, Dennis. *African Art and Literature: The Invisible Present*. London: Heinemann, 1977.

_____. and Cosmo Pieterse, eds. *African Writers Talking*. London: Heinemann, 1972.

Duggan, J. *Oral Literature: Seven Essays*. New York: Barnes and Noble, 1975.

Dundes, Alan. ed. *The Study of Folklore*. New Jersey: Prentice Hall, 1965.

_____. *Analytic Essays in Folklore*. New York: Mouton Publishers, 1975.

_____. "Metafolklore and Oral Literary Criticism," *The Monist* 50 (1966), 505-516.

Echeruo, Michael J.C. "The Dramatic Limits of Igbo Ritual," *Research in African Literatures* 4, i (1973), 21-31.

_____. "Igbo Thought Through Igbo Proverb: A Comment." *Conch* III, Vol. 2 (1971), 63-66.

_____. and E.N. Obiechina, eds. *Igbo Traditional Life, Culture and Literature*. Owerri, Nigeria: Conch Magazine Limited, 1971.

Egudu, R.N. "Social Values and Thought in Traditional Literature: The Case of the Igbo Proverb and Poetry," *Nigerian Libraries* 8, No. 2 (1972), 63-84.

_____. "Igbo Traditional Poetry and Family Relationships," *African Studies*, 32, No. 1 (1973), 15-24.

_____. "The Emotional Elements in Traditional Oral Poetry: The Igbo Experience," *Oral Poetry in Nigeria*, eds. Abalogu, Ashiwaju, and Amadi-Tshiwala. Lagos: Nigeria Magazine, 1981, 247-257.

_____ and Donatus Nwoga. *Igbo Traditional Verse*. London: Heinemann, 1973.

Ejiofor, L.U. *Igbo Kingdoms, Power and Control*. Onitsha: Africana Publishers Ltd., 1982.

Elliott, Robert C. *The Power of Satire: Magic, Ritual, Art*. New Jersey: Princeton University Press, 1960.

Encyclopaedia Britannica: Macropaedia. 1992 ed.

Enekwe, Ossie. "The Modern Nigerian Theatre: Which Tradition?" *Nsukka Studies in African Literature* 1, i (1978), 26-43.

Fage, J.D. *A History of West Africa*. London: n.p., 1969.

Feinberg, Leonard. *Introduction to Satire*. Ames, Iowa: The Iowa
      State University Press, 1967.

Feldman, B. and R.D. Richardson. *The Rise of Modern Mythology*.
      Bloomington: Indiana University Press, 1972.

Fergusson, F. *Aristotle's Poetics*. New York: Hill and Wang, 1961.

Finnegan, Ruth. *Oral Literature in Africa*. Oxford: Clarendon Press,
      1970.

_____. *Limba Stories and Story-Telling*. Oxford: Clarendon Press,
      1967.

_____. "How to do Things with Words: Performance Utterances
      Among the Limba of Sierra-Leone," *MAN* 4 (1964), 537-552.

Forde, Daryll. *African Worlds: Studies in the Cosmological Ideas and
      Social Values of African Peoples*. London: Oxford University
      Press, 1954.

_____ and G.I. Jones. *The Ibo and Ibibio-Speaking Peoples of
      Eastern Nigeria*. Oxford: Oxford University Press, 1950.

Fortes, Meyer and Germaine Dieterlen, eds. *African Systems of
      Thought*. London: Oxford University Press, 1965.

Fowler, Roger. *A Dictionary of Modern Critical Terms*. London:
      Routledge, 1973.

Fraser, Douglas and Herbert M. Cole, eds. *African Art and Leadership*.
      Madison: University of Wisconsin Press, 1972.

Freud, Sigmund. *Wit and its Relation to the Unconscious*. Trans.
      Abraham Arder Brill. New York: n.p., 1916.

_____. *Beyond the Pleasure Principle*, Trans. James Strachey. New
      York: Bantam, 1972.

Frye, Northrope. *Anatomy of Criticism: Four Essays*. New Jersey:
      Princeton University Press, 1973.

Gleason, Judith. "Out of the Irony of Words," *Transition* 18 (1965),
      34-38.

Gluckman, Max. *Custom and Conflict in Africa*. Glencoe, Illinois:
      The Free Press, 1955.

Goldstein, K.S. *A Guide for Field Workers in Folklore*. Hatboro:
      Folklore Associates, 1964.

Green, M.M. *Igbo Village Affairs*. London: Frank Cass and Co. Ltd.,
      1964.

Green, M. "Sayings of the Okonkwo Society of Igbo Speaking
      People," *Bulletin of the School of Oriental and African Studies*
      21 (1948), 838-846.

Green, R.C. *Tellers of Tales*. London: Kaye and Ward Ltd., 1969.

Griffiths, Gareth. "Language and Action in the Novels of Chinua Achebe," *African Literature Today* 5 (1971), 88-105.

Guiraud, Pierre. *Semiology*. London: Routledge and Kegan Paul, 1975.

Hanna, Judith Lynn. *To Dance is Human: A Theory of Nonverbal Communication*. Austin: University of Texas Press, 1979.

Heilman, Robert B. *The Ways of the World*. Seattle: University of Washington Press, 1978.

Henderson, Richard N. *The King in Every Man: Evolutionary Trends in Onitsha Ibo Society and Culture*. New Haven and London: Yale University Press, 1972.

Herskovits, Melville and Frances S. *Dahomean Narrative: A Cross-Cultural Analysis*. Evanston: Northwestern University Press, 1958.

Heywood, Christopher. *Perspective on African Literature*. London: Heinemann, 1971.

Highet, Gilbert. *The Anatomy of Satire*. Princeton: Princeton University Press, 1962.

Holman, C.H. and W. Harmon. *A Handbook to Literature*. New York: Macmillan Publishing Company, 1986.

Hopkins, Nicholas S. "Persuasion and Satire in the Malian Theatre," *Africa* 42, iii (1972), 217-228.

Hughes, Langston, ed. *An African Treasury*. New York: Crown, 1960.

Ifemesia, C. *Traditional Humane Living Among the Igbo*. Enugu: Fourth Dimension Publishers, n.d.

Ilogu, Edmund. *Christianity and Ibo Culture*. Leiden: E.J. Brill, 1974.

Isichei, Elizabeth. *A History of the Igbo People*. London: The Macmillan Press, 1976.

_____. *The Ibo and the Europeans*. London: Faber and Faber, 1973.

Jacobs, M. *The Content and Style of an Oral Literature*. Chicago: University of Chicago Press, 1959.

Jahn, Janheinz. *Muntu: An Outline of the New African* Trans. Marjorie Grene. New York: Grove Press, 1961.

Jones, G.I. *The Trading States of the Oil Rivers*. London: Oxford University Press, 1970.

Jordan, A.C. *Towards an African Literature: The Emergence of Literary Form in Xhosa*. Berkeley: University of California Press, 1973.

Jordan, John O. "Culture Conflict and Social Change in Achebe's *Arrow of God*," *Critique* 13, i (1970), 66-85.

Kalu, Ogbu. "Gods as Policemen: Religion and Social Control in

Igboland," *Religious Plurality in Africa*, eds. Jacob K.
Olupona and Sulayman S. Nyang. Berlin, New York: Mouton
de Gruyter, 1993, 109-131.

Kernan, Alvin. *The Plot of Satire*. New Haven: Yale University Press,
1965.

_____. *The Cankered Muse: Satire of the English Renaissance*. New
Haven: Yale University Press, 1959.

King, Bruce. ed. *Introduction to Nigerian Literature*. New York:
Africana, 1972.

Krappe, A.K. *The Science of Folklore*. London: Methuen, 1962.

Krohn, K.L. *Folklore Methodology*. Austin: American Folklore
Society, 1971.

Kuhn, Thomas S. *The Structure of Scientific Revolutions*, 2nd ed.
Chicago: Chicago University Press, 1970.

Kunene, Mazisi. "South African Oral Traditions." In *Aspects of South
African Literature*; ed. Christopher Heywood. London:
Heinemann, 1976.

_____. *Zulu Poems*. London: Andre Deutsch Limited, 1970.

Leach, M. "Problems of Collecting Oral Literature." In *Publication of
the Modern Language Association* 77 (1982), 335-530.

Lee, Charlotte I. *Oral Interpretation*. Boston: Houghton Mifflin Co.,
1952.

Leith-Ross, Sylvia. *African Women*. London: Routledge and Kegan
Paul Ltd., 1965.

Levine, Robert A. "Gusii Sex Offenses: A Study in Social Control,"
American Anthropologist 61 (1959), 965-990.

Leyburn, Ellen Douglas. *Satiric Allegory: Mirror of Man*. New
Haven, London: Oxford University Press, 1956.

Lindfors, Bernth. "Cultural Approaches to Folklore in African
Literature." In *African Folklore*, ed. Richard M. Dorson.
Bloomington: Indiana University Press, 1972, 223-234.

_____. *Folklore in Nigerian Literature*. New York: Africana
Publishing Co., 1973.

_____. "The Palm Oil With Which Achebe's Words are Eaten,"
African Literature Today 1 (1968).

_____. *Form of Folklore in Africa*. Austin: University of Texas
Press, 1977.

Lomax, Alan and Raoul Abdul, eds. *3000 Years of Black Poetry*. New
York: Dodd, Mead and Company, 1970.

Lord, A.B. *The Singer of Tales*. Cambridge: Harvard University Press,
1964.

Lystad, Robert A., ed. *The African World: A Survey of Social Research*. New York: Frederick A. Praeger, 1965.

Madumere, Adele. "Ibo Village Music," *African Affairs* 52 (1953), 63-67.

Mafeje, Archie. "The Role of the Bard in a Contemporary African Community," *Journal of African Languages* 6, iii (1967), 193-223.

Magill, Frank. *Masterpieces of World Literature*. New York: Harper & Row Publishers, 1960.

Majassan, A. "Folklore as an Instrument of Education Among the Yoruba," *Folklore* 8 (1969), 41-59.

Malinowski, Bronislaw. *The Dynamics of Culture Change: An Inquiry Into Race Relations in Africa*. Ed. Phyllis M. Kaberry. New Haven: Yale University Press, 1945.

Masterman, Margaret. "The Nature of a Paradigm." In *Criticism and the Growth of Knowledge*, eds. Lakatos, I. and Alan Musgrave. Cambridge: Cambridge Univ. Press (1970), 59-90.

Mbiti, John S. *African Religions and Philosophy*. London: Heinemann, 1969.

Merchant, W. Moelwyn. *Comedy*. London: Methuen Publishers, 1972.

Merton, R. and R. Nisbet, eds. *Contemporary Social Problem*. New York: Harcourt Brace, 1966.

Messenger, John C. "Ibibio Drama," *Africa* 41, iii (1971), 208-222.

Monye, Ambrose A. "Women in Nigerian Folklore: Panegyric and Satirical Poems on Women In Aniocha Igbo Oral Poetry." In *Power and Powerlessness of Women in West African Orality*, eds. Raol Granqvist and Nnadozie Inyama. Sweden: The Printing Office of Umea University, (1992), 63-74.

Murdock, P. *Our Primitive Contemporaries*. New York: The Macmillan Co., 1956.

Murray, K.C. "Dances and Plays," *Nigeria Magazine* 19 (1939), 214-218.

Mutwa, Credo. *My People*. London: Anthony Blond Ltd., 1969.

Mvula, Enoch S.T. "The Performance of Gule Wamkulu." In *The Oral Performance in Africa*, ed. Isidore Okpewho. Ibadan: Spectrum Books Limited, (1990), 80-97.

Newton-Smith, W.H. *The Rationality of Science*. London: Routledge and Kegan Paul, 1981.

Nicol, Eric. *In Darkest Domestica*. Toronto: The Ryerson Press, 1959.

Nicoll, Alardice. *An Introduction to Dramatic Theory*. New York: Brentano Publishing Company, 1931.

Noss, Philip A. "Description in Gbaya Literary Art." In *African Folklore*, ed. Richard M. Dorson. Bloomington: Indiana University Press, 1972.

Nwabueze, P. Emeka. "Igbo Masquerade Drama and the Origin of Theatre: A Comparative Synthesis," *KUNAPIPI* IX, 1 (1987), 89-97.

_____. "Igbo Masquerade Drama and the Problem of Alien Intervention: Transition from Cult to Theatre," *UFAHAMU* XIV, 1 (1985), 74-92.

_____. "Black Theatre in the African Continuum," *The Negro Educational Review* XXXVI, 2 (1985), 56-61.

_____. "The Masquerade as Hero in Igbo Traditional Society," *Frankfurter Afrikanistische Blatter* 1 (1989), 95-107.

Nwanunobi, C.O. *African Social Institutions*. Nsukka: University of Nigeria Press, 1992.

Nwaozuzu, B.S.C. "Igbo Folklore and Igbo World-view," *Nsukka Studies in African Literature* 3 (1980), 1-12.

Nwoga, D.I. "The Concept and Practice of Satire Among the Igbo," *The Conch* Vol. III, No. 2 (1971), 30-45.

_____. "The Igbo Poet and Satire." In *Oral Poetry in Nigeria*, eds. Abalogu, Ashiwaju and Amadi-Tshiwala. Lagos: Nigeria Magazine, (1981), 230-243.

_____ and R.N. Egudu. *Igbo Traditional Verse*. London: Heinemann, 1973.

Nzewi, Meki. "Some Social Perspectives of Igbo Traditional Theatre," *Black Perspectives in Music* Vol. 6, No. 2 (1978), 113-133.

_____. "The Rhythm of Dance in Igbo Music," *The Conch* Vol. III, No. 2 (1971) 104-108.

Obiechina, E.N. "Transition from Oral to Literary Tradition," *Presence Africaine* 63 (1967) 140-161.

Ogbalu, F.C. and E.N. Emenanjo, eds. *Igbo Language and Culture*. Ibadan: Oxford University Press, 1975.

Ohale, Christine N. "Women in Igbo Satirical Song." In *Power and Powerlessness of Women in West African Orality*, eds. Raol Granqvist and Nnadozie Inyama. Sweden: The Printing Office of Umea University, (1992), 33-42.

Okafor, C.A. "Research Methodology in African Oral Literature," *Okike* 16 (1979), 83-97.

Okeke, Ambrose N. "Traditional Education in Igboland." In *Igbo*

Language and Culture, eds. F.C. Ogbalu and E.N. Emenanjo. Ibadan: University Press Limited, (1982), 15-26.

Okoye, Pat U. *Widowhood: A Natural or Cultural Tragedy.* Enugu: Nucik Publishers, 1995.

Okpewho, Isidore, ed. *The Oral Performance in Africa.* Ibadan: Spectrum Books Limited, 1990.

_____. "Towards a Faithful Record: On Transcribing and Translating the Oral Narrative Performance." In *The Oral Performance in Africa*, ed. Isidore Okpewho, (1990), 111-135.

_____. *The Epic in Africa.* New York: Columbia University Press, 1979.

_____. *Myth in Africa: A Study of its Aesthetics and Cultural Relevance.* Cambridge: Cambridge University Press, 1983.

_____ ed. *The Heritage of African Poetry: An Anthology of Oral and Written Poetry.* Essex: Longman, 1985.

Osadebe, Oseloka O. "The Development of the Igbo Masquerader as a Dramatic Character." Ph.D. diss., Northwestern University, 1981.

Otten, Charlotte M., ed. *Anthropology and Art: Readings in Cross-Cultural Aesthetics.* New York: The Natural History Press, 1971.

Ottenberg, Simon. "Ibo Receptivity to Change." In *Continuity and Change in African Cultures*, eds. William R. Bascom and Melville J. Herskovits. Chicago: The University of Chicago Press, (1963), 130-143.

_____. *Anthropology and African Aesthetics.* Accra: Ghana University Press, 1971.

_____. "Afikpo Masquerades: Audience and Performers," *African Arts* 4, 4 (1973), 32-35, 94-96.

_____. "The Analysis of an African Play," *Research Review.* 7, 3 (1971), 66-84.

Owomoyela, Oyekan. "Folklore and Yoruba Theatre," *Research in African Literatures* 2, ii (1971), 121-133.

Parrinder, Georffrey. *African Traditional Religion.* London: Sheldon Press, 1974.

P'Bitek, Okot. *Song of Lawino.* Kenya: East African Publishing House, 1966.

Peek, P.M. "The Power of Words in African Verbal Arts," *Journal of American Folklore* 94 (1981), 19-43.

Peters, Helen. "Reflections on the Preservation of Igbo Folk Literature," *The Conch* Vol. III, No. 2 (1971), 97-103.

Pierson, William D. "Putting Down Ole Massa: African Satire in the New World," *Research in African Literatures* 7, 2 (1976), 166-180.

Potts, L.J. *Comedy*. London: Hutchinson's University Library, 1948.

Ramsaran, J.A. *New Approaches to African Literature*. Ibadan: Ibadan University Press, 1970.

Richards, I.A. *Practical Criticism: A Study of Literary Judgement*. London: Routledge and Kegan Paul, 1978.

Roscoe, A. *Mother is Gold: A Study in West African Literature*. Cambridge: Cambridge University Press, 1971.

Sackett, S.J. "Poetry and Folklore: Some Points of Affinity," *Journal of American Folklore* 77 (1964), 143-153.

Sannes, G.W. *African 'Primitives': Function and Form in Masks and Figures*. Trans. Margaret King. New York: Africana, 1970.

Schmidt, Nancy. "Nigerian Fiction and African Oral Tradition," *Journal of New African Literature and the Arts* 5, 6 (1968).

Sekoni, Ropo. "The Narrator, Narrative-Pattern, and Audience Experience of Oral Narrative Performance." In *The Oral Performance in Africa*, ed. Isidore Okpewho. Ibadan: Spectrum Books Limited, (1990), 139-159.

Sharman, Anne. "Joking in Padhola: Categorical Relationships, Choice and Social Control," *Man* 4, i (1969), 103-117.

Shelton, Austin J. "Relativism, Pragmatism, and Reciprocity in Igbo Proverbs," *The Conch* III, Vol. 2 (1971), 46-62.

———. "The Articulation of Traditional and Modern in Igbo Literature," *The Conch* I, (1969), 30-49.

Smith, W.W. ed. *The Artist in Tribal Society*. London: Routledge and Kegan Paul, 1961.

Soyinka, Wole. "Towards a True Theatre," *Nigeria Magazine* 75 (1962), 58-60.

———. *Myth, Literature and the African World*. London: Cambridge University Press, 1976.

———. *The Lion and the Jewel*. Oxford: Oxford University Press, 1963.

Starkweather, Frank. *Traditional Igbo Art: 1960*. Ann Arbor: Museum of Art, University of Michigan, 1968.

Steenberg, S.H. *Cassel's Encyclopaedia of World Literature*.

Stephenson, Robert C. "Farce as Method." In *Comedy: Meaning and Form*, ed. Robert W. Corrigan. Scranton: Chandler Publishing Co., (1965), 317-326.

Sutherland, James R. *English Satire*. Cambridge: University Press,

1962.

Talbot, Percy A. *The Peoples of Southern Nigeria*. London: Oxford University Press, 1926.

Thompson, Robert Farris. *African Art in Motion: Icon and Act*. Los Angeles: University of California Press, 1974.

Toman, W. *Family Constellation: Its Effect on Personality and Social Behaviour*. New York: Springer Publishing Co. Inc., 1969.

Tracy, Hugh. *Chopi Musicians: Their Music, Poetry, and Instruments*. London: Oxford University Press, 1958.

Traore, Bakary. *The Black African Theatre and its Social Functions*. Trans. Dapo Adelugba. Ibadan: University Press, 1972.

Tschumi, R. *Theory of Culture*. New York: Nok Publishers, 1978.

Turner, Victor. *The Forest of Symbols: Aspects of Ndembu Ritual*. New York: Cornell University Press, 1967.

Uchendu, Victor. *The Igbo of Southeast Nigeria*. New York: Holt, Rinehart and Winston, 1965.

Ugonna, Nnabuenyi. "Igbo Satiric Art: A Comment." In *Igbo Language and Culture*, Vol. 2, eds. Ogbalu and Emananjo. Ibadan: University Press Ltd., (1982), 65-79.

_____. Mmonwu: *A Dramatic Tradition of the Igbo*. Lagos: Lagos University Press, 1984.

Umeasiegbu, N.R. *The Way We Lived*. London: Heinemann, 1969.

Utley, Lea Francis. "Oral Genres as a Bridge to Written Literature." In *Folklore Genres*, ed. Dan Ben-Amos. Austin: University of Texas Press, (1969), 3-15.

Vansina, Jan. *Oral Tradition*. Trans. H.M. Wright. London: Routledge and Kegan Paul, 1965.

Worcester, David. *The Art of Satire*. New York: Russell, 1940.

INDEX

ABOUT THE AUTHOR

Christine Nwakego Ohale, née Oti, was born in Ihiala, near Onitsha, in Anambra State of Nigeria, and is a graduate of the University of Nigeria, Nsukka. She has been educated in Nigeria and the United States and holds two Master's degrees in English, and a Ph.D. in African Literature.

Dr. Ohale was, until her relocation to the United States, a Senior Lecturer in English at the University of Nigeria at Nsukka, a career that spanned roughly two decades, from 1981 to 2000. In 2000, she was a Visiting Scholar at the African Humanities Institute Programmes at the University of Ghana, Legon, and at Northwestern University, Evanston, Illinois, U.S.A. She has published essays in international journals in Africa, Europe, and the United States. At present, she is an Associate Professor of English at Chicago State University. Dr. Ohale lives in Chicago with her children.

Printed in the USA
CPSIA information can be obtained
at www.ICGtesting.com
LVHW010420251023
762071LV00004B/192